D1549541

GRANDPARENTING FOR THE NINETIES

BY ROBERT ALDRICH M.D. & GLENN AUSTIN M.D.

ROBERT ERDMANN PUBLISHING
INCLINE VILLAGE, NEVADA

Published by Robert Erdmann Publishing
28629 Meadow Glen Way West
Escondido, CA 92026
Telephone: (619) 749-3434
Fax: (619) 749-7689

Printed in the United States of America
First Printing

ISBN 0-945339-11-9 (Hardcover)

Library of Congress 90-082 830

CONTENTS

PREFACE

This book is about grandparenting. It includes everyone in the grandparents' generation, whether they have grandchildren of their own or not. The nation's most essential future resource is its children and all adults share the responsibility for their well being. We carry out this responsibility better by increasing our knowledge about the needs of children and their parents and the ways grandparents can help meet these needs. This is our purpose in writing this book — to offer some practical and effective ways to grandparent in the modern American society of the 1990s.

Our years of pediatric practice and teaching have exposed us to many strengths and some weaknesses in American families. One major problem is the relative loss of power by many parents who feel unable to control their children. Parents who know how to inculcate values and control their children while nurturing their confidence, produce more competent children. This reduces the risk of accidents and of dangers as diverse as drug abuse or academic underachievement. One reason for the widespread feeling of powerlessness among parents is the absence of grandparents who, with the advantage of experience, the successes and failures in raising their own children, could help guide and support parents. Instead, parents are often forced to choose between competing child-raising theories and experts. Rather than depend on theories, no matter how elegantly projected, we decided that the best model would be the experience of *successful* parents. We have seen a lot of successful rational-authoritative parents produce competent, confident and socially responsible adults.

In describing the model parent we had help from one of the few long-term scientific studies on how children turned out when raised by different parenting methods. Diana Baumrind followed the same group of families for thirty years. She objectively recorded the styles of parenting and the outcome of the children in her studies at the Institute of Human Development in the University of California at Berkeley. Dr. Baumrind allowed the use of her mostly unpublished research findings in the book, *Love and Power/Parent and Child*, by Dr. Austin. In the process we became aware that the experience of raising their own children led a lot of grandparents to naturally develop successful rational-authoritative methods. We call this style of parenting by grandparents, sensible grandparenting. It represents a lot of grandparental wisdom — and it needs to be put to use.

The growing needs of children have become a major national issue in America. President George Bush showed his concern in his first State of The Union address by calling upon grandparents to help meet the needs of the nation's children. The goal of this book is to show how active grandparenting benefits our grandchildren and strengthens the American Family. Grandparents' love and attention is especially needed in this day and age when so many parents have relatively little time with their children. Parenting is forever, and grandparents can routinely be a significant source of help for the whole family in both good times and bad.

The need to put grandparenting wisdom to work in helping parents raise their children runs up against the fragmentation of the American family. Solutions require more than advice to grandparents and parents; they also require broad social policy changes. Dr. Aldrich, as the originator of The Kid'sPlace Program currently spreading throughout the world, is effectively changing social policy. We teamed up to produce this book in order to help grandparents help their grandchildren and to focus national attention on the need for the extended family. We believe that the elders of America, with or without grandchildren, will see the necessity to help today's parents and children prepare for the formidable problems of the next century.

Robert A. Aldrich, M.D.   *Glenn Austin, M.D.*
Seattle, Washington   *Los Altos, California*

1 THE GRANDPARENTS ROLE: CLOSING THE LOOP

THE CHALLENGE

For the first time in memory a sitting President has linked the role of grandparents to the well-being of the country. President George Bush in his 1990 State of The Union address said:

> *". . .I'm going to ask something of every one of you.*
> *Let me start with my generation — the grandparents*
> *out there. You are our living link to the past. Tell*
> *your grandchildren the story of the struggles waged,*
> *at home and abroad. Of sacrifices freely made for*
> *freedom's sake. And tell them your own story as well*
> *— because every American has a story to tell."*

Why did he sound this stirring note? Is it because he and his wife, Barbara, are excellent grandparents themselves? More likely as a grandparent and a leader he understands the high hopes and appreciates the vivid expectations that young people have for their future — and which he shares as their President. But he knows that hope must be tempered with reality; lessons from the past must be heeded or past errors will be repeated. Experience has taught most grandparents some of the reasons for the differences between what is and what might be. Youth has yet to learn why society is not perfect, nor do they fully appreciate the struggles which brought the progress we now enjoy.

Grandparents can share their perspectives about how the world got to where it is today. They already know that great expectations and superb motives are not always enough to produce desired results. Like a mother robin carefully dropping a morsel of food into the wide open mouth of her newly hatched chick, grandparents provide morsels of truth for the waiting mind of the child. The President, wisely, has called for the renewal of this ancient relationship which has served mankind well during its evolution.

The aim of this book is to increase the ability of grandparents to help today's children succeed, to make their hopes and dreams come true. Events in Eastern Europe brilliantly demonstrate the force of the youth driven movement for freedom, peace and prosperity. When aided and abetted by elders, their drive becomes irresistible. Yet when the elders didn't help, for example when they failed to join their youth in the People's Republic of China, the drive collapsed. A natural alliance between youth and the elder generations must exist if we are to succeed in improving our world. President Bush astutely and optimistically reminded us of our traditional role in the lives of youth.

Cause For Optimism

We have good reason to be optimistic about the role of grandparents in American society. Our increasing knowledge about the effects of various forms of parenting, studies of families in other cultures, and thoughtful writings exploring the relationships of older citizens to children and youth all indicate a major role for grandparents. David Elkind's recent book, *Grandparenting: Understanding Today's Children*, is a good example. So is the existence of The Foundation For Grandparenting, dedicated to showing the importance of the grandparent-grandchild bond. The direct and valued historical relationship between elders and children fosters a positive evolution for mankind and has served human beings splendidly for thousands of years.

We believe this special bond between young and old will strengthen in the near future, reversing the late 20th century trend of families to drift apart. The population of the current grandparent generation is expanding rapidly, soon to be boosted even further by the middle aged "baby boom" generation following close behind us. The sheer numbers alone tell us that grandparents can have a major effect on this world. The effect will primarily consist of countless millions of small episodes where the elders make themselves available to children and youth. These episodes may be of even more importance when grandparents are not around, as it was for Adam:

Adam

Adam's grandparents are separated from him and his family by the thousands of miles between his house and the West Coast. One day his kindergarten class set a day at school for grandparents to visit. A retired neighbor across the street, whose white hair and ruddy cheeks framed his twinkling blue eyes, was Adam's friend. So, Adam sought him out and invited him to come to school and be his grandfather that day. The invitation was accepted with delight and that experience is now a neighborhood legend.

Young children seem to have an affinity and need for friendship with elders. These feelings are nearly always returned by the older person. Examples abound. Young high school girls and boys working in nursing homes for the elderly have been highly successful in stimulating the older folks to read, write poetry, make music and tell stories. Both young and old benefit from such mutual caring and respect. Sally, now in her fifties, clearly remembers how she sought out her elderly neighbors.

Sally

Sally's father had left so her mother had to work all day in a bakery to support the family. The town was small so people didn't worry too much about what the children would do when they got home from school. Eight-year-old Sally spent a good amount of time in the kitchen after school, learning to cook on her own. She found that she needed to borrow a cup of sugar, or get some advice, so she started visiting those neighbors who were home. Briget, a grey haired sixty-four-year-old woman, lived a couple of houses down the street. She really enjoyed Sally and would often serve tea and cookies as well as conversation and advice about making cookies. Sally still remembers how comforting it was to her to have a friend like Briget. She still enjoys the elderly and always looks for ways to help them.

Grandparents have more going for them than numbers. They are connected to their grandchildren by both biology and kinship, two of the most powerful links between human beings. An intimate acquaintance between grandchildren and grandparents closes the human family loop, reinforcing long standing basic values of our society, stabilizing families and assuring continuity during an era of rapid change in America.

GRANDPARENTS AND EVOLUTION

Today's grandparents have lived through more exciting times and have experienced more change than any generation before us. We benefited from the good and brave things our ancestors did to better the human condition. Especially in America, the shapers of society, the explorers and thinkers, the fighters and diplomats, the leaders and their followers bequeathed us a remarkable world. Certainly they also left us problems, but even our economic depressions seem like prosperity to much of the rest of the world, both historically and in our own times. Immigrants still flock to our shores with a passion for freedom and the promises it holds.

As the elders of our society we appreciate that passion; we helped defend that freedom. We each have much to be thankful for and a lot to pass on to the next generation. But we also have an obligation to look at the problems we inherited and the difficulties we bequeath to the future. We need to look honestly at not only our own state of being, but also at that of our children and grandchildren. Many causes for concern exist. While we successfully struggled out of depression and wars our generation prospered, but many children in America still live in poverty. While great advances have been forged in technology, some moral and practical values seem to have been lost.

The United States, unhappily, leads the world in the purchase and use of illegal drugs, has the highest rate of illegitimate pregnancy among the industrialized nations, and seems to be losing ground in education, production and environmental protection. While material prosperity has continued to inch forward for most American families, it is often at the expense of more and more mothers working outside the home and leaving their children in day care. Moving, spurred on by the frantic chase for job advancement and a better life, fragments families and weakens the ties between generations. Our grandchildren stand in danger of losing their roots. They inherit problems as well as progress.

The Way Things Were

Most grandparents can recall their life in the villages, towns and cities where they were raised — where grandparents lived in the household and took part in the regular duties of the home. Or they were close by so that a visit to Grandma's home could be made just any time of day. You could hop on your bicycle after school and ride over to feed the chickens or see if the radishes you planted in her garden had started to come up. The many memories warm us. For example, sixty-year-old Olive remembers herself as a three-year-old who couldn't get her busy mother's attention.

Her Mother had just put the baby and two-year-old Everett down for a nap, washed the dirty diapers on the washboard in the tub, and was hanging them on the clothes line. Olive, a bit put out by the combined competition of her younger brothers and the necessary wash, decided she could get more attention from Grandma and made the two mile trip on her own. In this sparsely settled part of the New England countryside the road to Grandma's cut through a thick forest which wore bright Autumn reds and yellows. She had the empty road to herself and her companion, a small bulldog named Mickey who decided to accompany her as she trudged along. Her thoughts were not on the Autumn beauty but more about sitting on Grandma's lap, getting hugs and kisses from her aunts and uncles and possibly a fresh juicy McIntosh apple from the apple tree in their front yard.

As Olive turned the last bend in the road someone from Grandma's farm house spotted her, and startled, ran to meet her. Just as they reached Olive, her mother, with baby in one hand and leading Everett with the other, panted around the bend and caught up with her. Olive's bravery left her for a moment as she wondered if she might get spanked because she seemed to have upset everyone; instead both Mother and Grandmother hugged her as if she had been lost forever.

CHANGES

Childhoods such as Olive's, during the depression of the 1930s were not too bad for most. There was enough to eat even though government welfare didn't exist. Growing up during those troubled times taught the value of work and of saving. College was not for everybody and lots of young people who went worked their way through. Then came World War II when 12 million men went off to the Service while their places in the factories were filled by Rosie the Riveter. Women proved themselves to be the equal of men in the work place; things have never been the same since. When the men came back, often with brides from distant states or foreign countries, it was to a prosperous, confident but restless society. Families moved as better job opportunities were offered in distant cities. The nuclear family of mother, father and child became the norm. The extended family network was broken as many adult children married and moved away from their family.

Against a background threat of nuclear holocaust and the economic drain of fighting the cold war against communism came the Korean war, recessions, and then Vietnam and the assassination of President John F. Kennedy. The guns and butter policy of President Johnson's administration sparked inflation and great discontent, especially among the youth who were called on to go to Vietnam to fight a strange war for an uncertain cause in an unfamiliar land. Their restlessness partially stemmed from living in isolated nuclear families without the structure and support or the widely accepted values that most of today's grandparents grew up with. The tranquility of the nation was shaken further by the Watergate scandal. Youth, rebellious as always and cynical about the state of the world, given the freedom of the pill and having more money than experience, turned first to rock music, then to punk, then to heavy metal while many of them experimented with sex and drugs. In spite of this the great majority grew up and developed into admirable, competent and socially responsible citizens. We were their parents. We were with them. Most of us still wonder how, as parents, we did as well as we did in those turbulent times.

PARENTING WITHOUT HELP

Many families had lost the close association with grandparents. The network of the extended family weakened with the massive movement and reshuffling of the population leaving grandparents and other relatives behind. It left much of society solely dependent on the integrity of the nuclear family of Mother, Father and Child. It left too many nuclear families isolated, without the support or counsel of grandparents.

One of the results of the lack of readily available grandparents was that parents were often uncertain about how to handle the many normal situations they faced raising their children. As a result they looked for and turned to experts in child rearing. But the experts didn't really exist. A publisher, recognizing the need and desire of parents for guidance, asked pediatrician Ben Spock to fill the gap. Dr. Spock at that time was one of the few pediatricians who had seriously studied psychiatry. He used the psychiatric theory of his day to guide him in writing his first book in 1948, *The Common Sense Book of Baby and Child Care*. Parents, lonely and insecure, away from the guidance of their own parents, eagerly grasped the easily available pocket book. Grandparents often were not as readily available, their advice and counsel was harder to come by and they were not professionals, so their advice was largely shelved. Lost with it were deeper American values that come more from personal human experience than from reading pocket books. Thus a new path in the evolution of child rearing was established.

Spock's book has been followed by a deluge of books, often conflicting, advising parents how to raise their children. Psychologists, social workers and child development specialists flooded society with their advice. Significant increases in understanding and much good comes from the work of these myriad counselors and health workers. But much of their work is based on complex tenuous theories rather than practical experience and has, as a result, produced a good amount of misleading information. One psychiatrist candidly cautioned parents that although his book was based on the most up to date psychiatric theory, in ten years it would be obsolete. But parents have to raise their children in the here-and-now. So they used what they could, both the good and the shaky advice.

The cult of permissiveness, springing from a theory about how to raise children, was largely a reaction to the problems created by harsh authoritarian child rearing. It cannot really be blamed on Spock. Rather it was an amorphous, well-intended social movement away from the extremes of authoritarian child rearing, spurred on by moral revulsion to the tyranny and brutality of fascism and communism. Much like the rebellion of 1989 in Eastern Europe, the indignation against the suppressive overuse of authority colored the attitudes of parents and was a major factor in the growth of more permissive child-rearing and the relative permissiveness of society. Human nature, being what it is, welcomed the concept of freedom without much clearly defined responsibility. For awhile it seemed obtainable, and values changed.

CHANGING VALUES

Social permissiveness, aided by the pill which assured birth control, encouraged the sexual revolution with its plague of venereal diseases and its splintering effect on families. At the same time the increased psychological awareness of the need for high self-esteem indirectly increased the self-centered tendency of many people. Divorce rates soared. Lack of social structure, particularly in the 1960's, as well as the weakening of traditional values by permissiveness, left everyone to "do their own thing," widening the path to drug abuse, sexual abuse and personal irresponsibility, culminating in the spread of AIDS. Life, liberty and the pursuit of happiness permeates national thinking. However, millions began to learn that personal freedom includes the price of personal responsibility. Most grandparents, being products of the great depression, know this well and often desperately want to protect their children and grandchildren from the price of ignoring established family values.

In spite of the need, many grandparents feel unable to approach their grandchildren or fear their advice is unwanted or will go unheeded, so they do not offer it. Some of this feeling of being useless and discarded comes from the emergence of child-care "experts" who challenged the child rearing practices of the past. The increasing problems of society seemed to give credence to these challenges, sowing doubt among parents, now today's grandparents. Even though today's grandparents improved the world for their children and grandchildren compared to the prior century, societal problems have continued to increase. Lack of structure, lack of belonging, and confusion about one's role contributed to the personal unhappiness of many people. Professionals looking for the root causes of this unhappiness attribute many problems to the way individuals were parented. Thus "parent bashing" has become the order of the day, largely directed at today's grandparents.

In some cases the blame is certainly justified. But the overall effect has been to make even many good parents defensive and insecure. Parenting has become a chore to many because the individual autonomy, power and self-respect of parents has been challenged as never before. Parental insecurity, aggravated by the emergence of parenting experts, in itself reduces parenting effectiveness.

Escape

Many grandparents found it easier to escape than to be involved. Due to Social Security, which improved their economic status and lessened their need to be financially dependent on their children, grandparents can look beyond the family for other challenges. This tendency was increased by the prevailing attitude, a drumbeat of criticism from the child-rearing experts, implying that grandparents had failed as parents. Criticism of parents has not decreased even though some of the failures once attributed by psychological theory to parenting errors were later discovered by medical research to have been due to genetic biochemical diseases, for example some alcoholism, depression and schizophrenia.

Some of today's grandparents still believe, underneath it all, that they are responsible for many of the problems and difficulties their children and grandchildren experience. Some are. This feeling has been a major factor in the development of the grandparent's attitude that, "I've done my duty. I shouldn't butt in on my adult child's parenting." It is a tacit admission of the uncomfortable feeling that they didn't do as good a job of parenting as they might have done, as well as their innate respect for their adult-child's turf. Such attitudes fuel the segregation of society by age, evidenced by the proliferation of walled-off adult-only communities, apartment buildings and nursing homes. But grandparents are not the only ones feeling disenfranchised from their children. Today's mothers face the same problems and it tends to drive them from their children.

Continuing parental insecurity contributes to the widespread phenomenon of the women's movement and to the devaluation of mothers at home. With all of these forces at work many parents find it easier to escape than to be involved. In *Kids First Newsletter,* from

Calgary Canada, writer Nancy Devlin reported a study showing that being a mother and homemaker is more stressful than working outside the home. She offered the following comment:

"One of the reasons for this might be that a woman's role in the marketplace is more easily defined and can be measured as being productive, while the role of mother, especially that of new mother, can be characterized as flying by the seat of your pants with no real guidelines, but with lots of guilt and little feeling of accomplishment. This is especially true in today's world because new mothers no longer have a support network of relatives and friends to assist them and to serve as role models to them.

"A new mother is a very vulnerable creature. She reads books by experts who tell her what to do and not to do. Since many so-called experts disagree, the new mother is faced with making a choice but is told that there are dire consequences if she guesses wrong. Many would be happy to trade this uncertainty for the certainties of a career outside of the home."

Another effect of the escape from home, of the splintering of families, is the damage it does to teenagers. They especially are threatened by uncertainty in their societal environment — the lack of a solid social structure and accepted values in the United States. Their instinctive challenge to society has, in the past, been controlled to a degree by traditional social structure. Somehow we must learn which social structures nurture the maximum healthy growth and development of teenagers into socially responsible productive human adults. We know that adolescents raised in a small town with commonly accepted values, with a common religion and a defined path to tread, have fewer problems. Teenagers do well in suburbs characterized by a common social structure and values, reported researcher Francis A.J. Inanni, in his book, *The Search for Structure: A Report On American Youth Today.* Each stage of human development undoubtedly has its own requirements. Just as we are learning about the needs of the fetus and the infant, so must we look at each stage of human development. We should also find the roles grandparents can play and the contributions they can make at different stages of development.

The combination of parental insecurity and geographical splintering of family networks tends to remove grandparents from the family loop. This unfortunate conjunction of affairs occurs at a time of impending crisis, at a time when the mutual support of a family network can be invaluable. During change and crisis the security and support of family enables individuals to meet challenges more efficiently and confidently. And as the 20th Century draws to a close it appears that the challenges and changes will increase.

CHANGE AND CRISIS

We bequeath major problems to our grandchildren and great grandchildren. Our earth, our society, is in crisis. George Kennan, emeritus professor at Princeton and former ambassador to the Soviet Union, called attention to two great dangers of this age:

"One, that we end up destroying our civilization violently through lack of control over the weapons of mass destruction; and two, that we destroy it nonviolently — but none the less relentlessly — through our indifference and our lack of adequate response to the global environmental crisis that is so clearly advancing upon us. . . If we can believe even half of what we hear from highly qualified scientific sources, then we — with our relentless overpopulation, our pollution of air, water and soil, and our reckless depletion of non-renewable resources — are rapidly wearing out the capacity of our rich, beautiful, and unique planet to sustain humanity."

We share George Kennan's assessment of the future. It can be an exciting and fulfilling time, but warning signals have been sent up for decades by astute observers in the sciences, industrial leaders, politicians and concerned citizens. This strikes home on a smoggy day in Los Angeles or Mexico City when we can't run as fast or breath as well as we could when the air was clean. To detect toxic air in the coal mines the miners carried canary birds with them. The little birds were more easily overcome by toxic gasses than were the miners. When the birds keeled over it was a signal for the miners to leave. A newspaper reported from Mexico City that a caged canary placed on the planted median between two lanes of traffic on a major boulevard lasted only twenty minutes before being overcome.

The damage humans do to and suffer from the environment is not encouraging. Limits very likely exist to the amount of environmental damage beyond which we dare not go without adversely influencing the future of mankind — the future of our grandchildren. Humans have a duel role on our planet. We are both the instigators of change and we and our grandchildren either benefit or suffer from the change. We face a possibility that we may create an environment in which man cannot survive. To avoid this requires experience, maturity and wisdom.

One cannot expect young adults to have the same store of experience, maturity and wisdom as their elders. This experience must not be lost. We learn from history or we repeat its mistakes. We all know some of the mistakes which could lead to Kennan's postulated relentless destruction of civilization. We can add to the list of foreseeable problems which may effect our grandchildren in the future from depleted ozone in the sky, depleted forests in the Amazon, the greenhouse effect and weather changes, to the suburban sprawl which puts homes on what was once prime food producing land in America. Having lived through premature predictions that the world will run out of oil in our time we might feel that Kennan and the bevy of alarmed scientists are like the boy who called wolf too often. But we should remember that the wolf finally did come! Perhaps the most threatening wolf that our grandchildren will face is not the nuclear bomb but the population bomb.

The Population Bomb

Recent space probes by the Voyager space ship provided evidence that there is no place else to live in our solar system. For survival, we had better make the best of what we have here on earth. This means no less than the planet itself with all of its flora and fauna including mankind. In an unfilled planet when the population was small, population growth could be accommodated by migration to new areas. Now worldwide shortages of energy, food, and clean water appear on the horizon. Dr. Jonas Salk, in his perceptive book, *The Survival of the Wisest*, compared world population dynamics to the dynamics of yeast cells growing in a closed system. When they grow enough to use up their food their growth slows down. Recent evidence shows a slowing of the rate of the world population growth. Is our population, like yeast in a test tube, facing survival problems because of lack of space, lack of energy, lack of food?

Our planet is a closed system. What is here is here. The earth is not being renewed from some outer source with water, land, air and life. It is also evident that there is no other place to go in this solar system. Another solar system? Maybe yes, but a long time from now. Meanwhile, data from the United Nations Population Fund shows that the estimated rate of world population growth has been slowing for several years. The numbers of the world population continue to rise, but the *rate* of increase is slowing. Still, China's attempt to control its population over the past decades failed; they went over their planned population by 200,000,000 people, almost as many as the population of the United States! Over half of China's population is under the age of thirty years and half of Mexico's population is under the age of fifteen years with massive implications for population growth. Yet current trends suggest that space, energy, food and environmental pressures will reduce population growth to zero by the year 2095. It may be, then, that Dr. Salk's concept is one of the new realities driving the changes we are beginning to experience.

Assuming that human ingenuity and a spirit of cooperation can solve many of the ecological problems facing mankind, and our great-grandchildren manage to have enough food, water, clean air, energy and adequate waste disposal, then what happens? Studies have been done in rat colonies which were furnished with all these necessities so their population kept increasing, but they were kept in the same limited space. With increased population growth the animals soon began suffering from the effects of crowding. They became neurotic, their family structure broke down and some of them acted almost psychotic. The implication is that hard choices will have to be made by humans in our planet of limited space. There are many reasons for what is taking place in the world. Some are beyond our control but others are within our grasp if we act. This requires, at the very least, changes in both our style of living and our values.

CHANGE AND VALUES

These challenges require change. We *will* change because when survival becomes a human issue the usual values of society change. This occurs in wars, rebellions, or catastrophes of nature. People trying to survive will abandon some of the values they live by under normal circumstances and adopt new values which will help their survival. If catastrophes, supplies or space do not limit the population, the birth rate and family size will have to decrease. That is not easy. What will upcoming generations be faced with? What resources will they have to work with? How will they provide food, shelter and work for the expanding population of the world? Will they be able to protect their environment from toxic wastes? Their future is in question today.

The primary issue emerging in the next decades is survival. It had seemed that nuclear war between the great powers was the most terrifying threat. At least this threat seems to be receding even if it has not gone away. But looming before every human being on earth is a basic problem, preserving our planet in a condition that allows us to survive. We are indeed in a survival struggle. Survival of the fittest is a slogan we are all more or less familiar with. It is something we often take for granted as "great truth." Basically, it means that the most competitive or strongest "winner" takes all. Competition has become a prime value — one of the principal guides to American behavior. It is a comfortable way to live when the resources of the planet are sufficient to support the population.

Most of today's grandparents grew up under the belief system of unfettered competition. Yet if we look at the changes in society that bother most of us, many of them are partially created by competition. We increasingly express alarm about rising prices for certain services or commodities, shortages of housing, crowded cities, dangerous streets, criminality, corruption in business and government, erosion of the value of savings and investments through inflation and lack of government regulation. The solution to many of these problems, to the change from times of plenty to times of scarcity, may lie in cooperation rather than competition.

Some of the values prevalent during times of plenty are listed here in the left hand column, and in times of scarcity in the right hand column.

TIMES OF PLENTY	TIMES OF SCARCITY
Competition	Cooperation
Parts	Whole
Absolute	Balance
Power	Consensus
Independence	Interdependence
Individual	Group

It is our thought that certain values are necessary for survival in the face of shortages. Indeed, some of the changes we note in the world now reflect early movement from the values of plenty to the values of scarcity and survival. The shifts toward consensus and cooperation should be welcome replacements for increasingly outmoded competition. Even the United States Senate rose above its usual competitive partisan politics to pass a clean air bill to get the decade of the 1990s off to a good start. Powerful nations seem to be moving toward cooperation and consensus rather than competition, in both internal and international affairs. Japan, a crowded country with close to zero population growth, has one of the most cooperative and consensus oriented societies existing and has a remarkable record of success in production and trade. Their experiences, both positive and negative, may serve as a demonstration project for the rest of the world. Europe's Common Market offers another example of the move from often bitter competition to cooperation. Profound changes seem to be occurring, anticipating the realities of the future by acting to meet the problems of today. The grandparent generation President Bush addressed so eloquently will play a large role in seeing that values are appropriate for both our time and our grandchildren's time in the future. We had better make the best of what we have here on earth.

To carry out our role we will have to use the native intelligence given to mankind, coupling it to a vision of the future that draws upon the great minds of the past. We, as grandparents, each carry some of this intelligence and information and can offer our grandchildren personal entrance into the large store of wisdom generated by both ancient and modern cultures. From this, we and tomorrow's adults should be able to determine the best direction to take. Our role is not to raise children, we should concentrate on raising adults by helping children grow into responsible, competent, well-informed, mature individuals. Of course this is not just the responsibility of grandparents, but we do have a role and can play a significant part in exposing our grandchildren to solid survival values to ensure the continued evolution of mankind. In the process, grandparents survive and grow—we evolve.

THE EVOLUTION OF GRANDPARENTS

The evolution of mankind continues. Grandparents can help determine which direction it will take. The torch we pass on to our grandchildren, will light the way to the future. A good future requires that they learn the lessons of the past and avoid the mistakes we made. This task, to a considerable degree, falls on the shoulders of grandparents, for nothing replaces the impact of personal lessons from those who have lived the experiences. Thus, what we teach our grandchildren becomes a basis for their future. And in the process, we ourselves evolve — we improve our knowledge and abilities and so are better able to live up to our responsibilities to the future.

Constructive evolution avoids the errors and learns from the successes of history. The child benefits from exposure to the personal history of each grandparent — it can be a searing or a heartwarming experience to hear the defeats and the victories of your blood line. Grandparents are the roots, part of the gene pool, and forgers of the make-up of each grandchild. What counts most is the knowledge of the personal evolution of a grandparent, how the grandparent learned and benefited from experiences. A grandparent's objective view, even an emotional view, of what she or he did right or wrong, of what society did that was right or wrong, becomes an invaluable lesson to be passed on to future generations via the grandchildren. Most of us learned from our life experiences and many of us would do things differently if we but had the chance. We can tell this to our grandchildren who are keenly interested in what led to their current status in society as it now exists.

President Bush has good reason to advise grandparents to link up with American children and youth. Growing children and adolescents receive and integrate vast amounts of information about themselves, their family, society and the world. For them to use this information in a positive way they must understand history and learn solid values. Grandparents impart history and values by their very existence; it made the existence of their grandchildren possible. Thus most grandchildren realize that they have an obligation to listen. Also, grandparents, having been around awhile, have a better overall view of human growth and development than the young; this allows them to understand and teach more effectively. They know that each stage of life affords unique opportunities for the individual which may not bear fruit until a later stage in life. They recognize that damage done at one stage of life, be it physical, spiritual, intellectual or emotional, often creates problems at a later stage.

Sharing Our Heritage

A deep and passionate interest in her heritage kept 70-year old Mae Timbimboo's memories alive. The Associated Press reported her memories of sitting at the feet of her Shoshone grandfather in their cabin listening to his stories of past events while the chill winter winds moaned outside:

"He was the best story teller. He believed in passing his stories on to his grandchildren and he expected them to memorize all of them. We sat on the floor and Grandpa sat on the chair. Every few minutes he would ask, 'Are you awake? Are you awake?' she recalled.

"And we would say yes. If one of us fell asleep Grandpa would just get up and leave. So we stayed awake. He wanted us to know who we were and where we came from."

As good ancestors we need to understand our own strengths and weaknesses and pass this knowledge on to our grandchildren. This requires maturity, study and judgment. Maturity comes with time, experience and learning from that experience. The result is often wisdom. Wisdom and knowledge bring changes in our attitudes about raising children and our values. Usually this improves the parenting skills of grandparents. It's not that we, or our children as parents, did a bad job. But we have learned from our mistakes, and most of us made at least a few of those. We learned, and this knowledge as well as the knowledge of our successes, can now guide us as we approach our obligation to the future.

One of the greatest strengths of the elder generation comes from having reared our own children. Nothing matures a person as much as having children; nothing forces us to grow up as much. Our gray hair partially represents *the* ultimate experience — being a parent. Hundreds of books exist on how to raise children. Contrast this to the astonishing lack of books about how raising children causes the *parents* to grow up. We do grow, and this occupation represents one of the really major events in our life span. From conception on we continually change. Physically we grew in size during the first two decades. Our brain size grew rapidly in the uterus and during the first year of life, then slowly for the next few years. Our ability to learn and reason, our cognitive development, continues and often improves throughout life. Maturation and time generally improve our function, our social development and our personality.

Visualizing Personal Evolution

A model of different stages throughout human life is pictured in figure 1. You can use the illustration to visualize how an event at a specific age ends up influencing us at a later age. For example injury to the brain, say from drug abuse, may impair intellect, reasoning and success at a future stage of life. The figure would be clearer if it were three dimensional, water melon shaped, with each stripe representing a different aspect of life. Each stripe or line is related to and affects the other, and taken together offer a picture of the individual. We can visualize all of these facets, be they physical or psychological, coalescing to allow prediction of a person's future life trends. The model brings together the anthropological and biological aspects of man. It helps us to get a "feel" for where grandparents fit into Nature's scheme of things — the continuity of conception, birth, the joy of living, the wisdom of age gathered and passed on to the next generation and the release of death.

Figure 1
Human Life Span Development

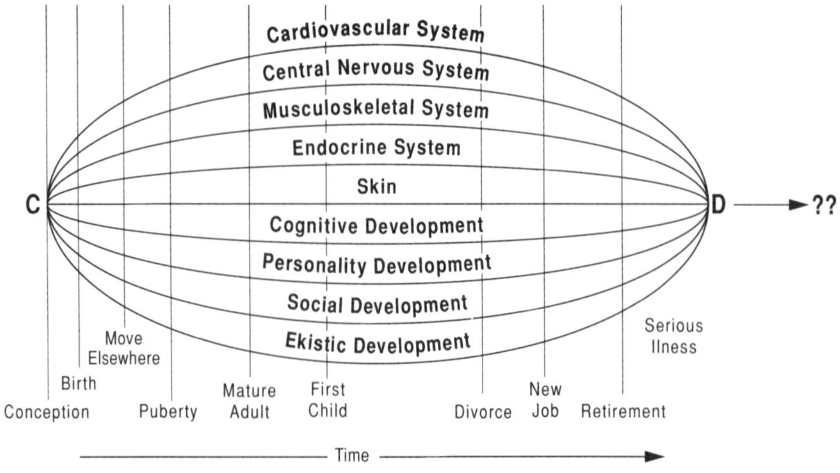

Mae Timbimboo appreciates how her grandfather fit into Nature's scheme of things. He provided lessons from the past, nurtured her and her sisters and brothers with attention, with demands, "Are you awake?" and disciplined them by leaving if they did not pay attention. Mae's sense of self-esteem, of belonging, of history and significance were fueled by her grandfather. Grandparents count, Mae's, your's, everybody's.

AN OLD FASHION SONG

Fortunately, progress in our knowledge about survival continues to accrue as the problems grow. For example we learned relatively recently that the alcohol effect on the unborn fetus creates the most common form of mental retardation in the United States. Alcohol used by pregnant women may deform the baby's face as well as cause mental retardation. Cocaine and other illicit drugs also produce damaged infants. This is avoidable. So is transmission of the dreaded virus of AIDS by infected blood, from sexual aberrations or the shared hypodermic needles of drug abusers. And out of the resulting intense research emerges a better understanding of human immunity. These examples remind us of the vulnerability of the fetus to damage from circumstances beyond it's control.

Alcohol, AIDS and cocaine represent customs of a segment of society that grandmothers may influence. The strong bond connecting the baby's grandmother to his mother allows personal education to be more effective than public education. Grandmothers can sometimes effectively urge new mothers to seek prenatal care, eat well and to avoid alcohol, drugs and venereal disease. This may sound like an old fashion song, but it holds the best advice for mother and child. It's worth a try. Grandmothers of the nation can make a major contribution by guiding their daughters and granddaughters. We *do* know what to do, but we are not doing it.

Closing the Loop

It is time that grandparents come off the shelf and resume their role and responsibilities as ancestors. In spite of the generic, and in many cases personal, criticism of their effectiveness as parents, most of today's grandparents did a better job than the critics realize. And whatever their effectiveness as parents, the maturation and wisdom which comes with age has improved them as individuals. Each grandparent offer's a personal and meaningful historical perspective of what led to their grandchild's state of being. Grandparents often have more time than the parents to spend with the children, offering the opportunity to pass on history and values. This allows the opportunity to teach, to lead, to increase the self-esteem and confidence, competence and social responsibility of their grandchildren. They even have the opportunity to improve the parenting they use on their adult children, as we will see in the following chapters.

The Challenge

We believe it fair to ask the grandparenting generation – are we being good ancestors? Are we doing all that we can to make the planet safe and productive for the next generation? Grandparents can be particularly valuable now if they focus on those values which will help the new generation prosper. Today's children and youth will be in charge of our affairs during the first part of the next century. This challenges us to join with them in a major international effort, uniting mankind to insure the survival of our species and continued evolution. This starts with each of us relating more closely and more meaningfully to our grandchildren.

On a personal basis each grandparent is part of the personal nurturing structure and social stability needed by each child. How close the relationship is depends on many factors varying from geography to personality to attitudes and values. But regardless of the difficulties, scratch the surface and you find the need for grandparents. Just as each child needs his parents, each child needs his own grandparents. No one can really replace an individual's grandparents. Nor do the needs of our children vanish into the mist when the children become competent and responsible adults. Parenting is forever. The value of family, the strength of the grandparent-parent-grandchild relationship remains intact. On the surface many of these relations have seemed to atrophy. But those who believe that have not seen or felt the emotional impact of a letter or call from grandmother. It is time to reach out and touch your children and grandchildren.

Becoming Involved

But how do you help? Arthur Kornhaber, M.D., in *Vital Connections, The Grandparenting Newsletter*, movingly wrote:

"Give of yourself. . . For most of human history, families slogged out rough times together. But increasingly we are witnessing an unprecedented splitting of the generations; grandparents from parents, parents from children; grandparents from grandchildren. The social and emotional repercussions of the rending asunder of families has resulted in something approaching social chaos.

"Your daughters are uniquely stressed. As mothers, they are torn between their heads and their hearts, their allegiance to their children and their need or desire to enter the work world. These women walk an emotional tightwire.

"And your sons are also striving to make it. There's a lot of pressure out there, pressure many of today's grandparents never had to deal with.

"Even you yourself might still be on the same treadmill that you were twenty years ago, waiting till the day that may never come to "take it easy."

"And what about your grandchildren?

"Many of us search for the perfect gift. Well, the perfect gift may be right under our noses. With all the social upheaval around these days, your family could probably use your help. And any holiday season might just be the time for you to look at what your family needs, and then to do something about it.

Dr. Kornhaber continues his sage advice. . . "How do we help? Simple. Ask your kids and your grandchildren what you can do for them. Indeed, ask your own parents too, if they are still around. Then do it. Even if its inconvenient, or if you feel intrusive, do it anyway. Myths that characterize grandparents as being "meddlesome" are just that: myths. If your family sees you that way, talk about it, then try to be more caring.

"If you have more than you need, share it with your kids with the understanding that they will help you in turn. Give your families the most time that you can. If you see something wrong, speak up and offer a constructive solution.

"Above all, don't stand as a silent witness to your family's suffering. We believe in a generation of grandparents that is active and vital. We should not be a generation of grandparents who will whine over what our children aren't doing for us. There's work to be done."

Dr. Kornhaber calls a spade a spade. There *is* work to be done. Luckily we can be optimistic that grandparents are up to meeting the challenge. The old phrase, "It is better to give than receive," still holds true. Even if your grandchildren are out of reach, the need and the opportunity exists to be a neighborhood or community grandparent. Start by getting to know your neighbors. Invite them over for tea. Learn about their lives and their children. This doesn't require being nosy, usually it just requires being a good listener. Ask if the parents will mind if you "hire" their children to help you weed the garden or wash your car. Once friendly relations are established you might volunteer to take the neighbor children to the zoo or a movie, or even to serve as a substitute when mother and father cannot make it to a PTA meeting or teacher's conference. Many of the parents in your own neighborhood probably miss their own parents and wish that their children had their own grandparents close by. The children need them. More such need exists than is usually expressed. You may find that you, like Adam's elderly neighbor, can serve as an admirable substitute. Parenting is forever, whether or not you can get to your own children and grandchildren. The course of evolution of society will, to a considerable degree, depend upon the amount and quality of grandparenting received by today's adults and children. We need to close the loop.

2   TIME WITH GRANDCHILDREN: MAKING IT PAY

A New Look at Grandparenting Methods: Trials & Errors, Theories & Research

Grandparenting involves more than the mutual love and security which comes with the role. Love alone is not enough. However, it does provide the stimulus to interact with grandchildren and the motivation to make that interaction a productive and positive experience. To do this requires time, high quality time, between grandparents and their grandchildren. Some have precious few minutes of such contact while others really function as the grandchild's parents. Either way we want to make our minutes enjoyable and our days pay off. One way is to help our grandchildren develop their competence, confidence, intelligence and social responsibility — to be the best and happiest they can be. Sounds like a big order, but a real opportunity exists for almost all grandparents to contribute to the development of their grandchildren. Children want and need guidance, discipline, structure, stimulation, freedom and fun as well as love. They need all of this, they need all the help they can get because they face intimidating personal and societal problems in this decade which will accelerate in the next century. Children will have to become competent adults.

Grandparents can contribute far more to the development of their grandchildren's competence than most people realize. Evidence from research indicates that some parenting methods produce far better results than others. Many if not most grandparents are well on their way to using these methods naturally and easily and, like you, continue to work toward even better "grand" parenting methods. An innate reward for all comes with such improvement — increasing one's effectiveness is always very satisfying.

One good way to improve our effectiveness is to look for good models and learn from them. Which form of child raising works best? Was it the one you used on your children or something you never experienced, used by a culture different than yours? Some of us still worry about the way we raised our now adult children. If we made mistakes, have we learned enough from them or do we just take antacids? Even if we did a good job, can we improve on it for our adult children and our grandchildren? But who do we learn from, the experts? Or maybe from other grandparents?

Trial and Error

Grandfather John Colton brought two-year-old Jimmy in for a check up; he took care of his grandson while his single-parent daughter worked. We asked for his advice about grandparenting. He thought it over, harrumphed and said, "I looked at parenthood as a somewhat trial and error process, and it's only when your kids grow to adulthood that you can properly evaluate what worked and what didn't work. This is helpful experience to draw on in helping raise a grandchild, but having said that, you have to remember that the parent is boss."

The trial and error process didn't start in a vacuum. John's parents immigrated from Europe and stressed the importance of character and self-reliance. He said, "I suspect that I will do what I can to stress these qualities in my grandson. I think Oriental families do this well and it's part of the reason for their success." It worked for Colton. Each of us experienced how we were raised and how we reacted to our parents and we carry this pattern within us. This experience, this inner child of the past, stays with us and often runs our lives. We tend to react to our children emotionally, based on our past experiences, more than logically. The same occurs with our grandchildren.

Even when reason asserts itself, emotions can stand in the way. John grinned and admitted, "At first I thought I would try to be a teacher to my two-year-old grandson, Ronald, so he would have a head start academically. I read a book that tells how to teach children to read at the age of two. I finally had to abandon this approach due to my lack of patience and Ronald's very active nature. I've switched to the learn by playing approach."

The lessons John learned from childhood helped him to become a very successful man. But the stress his parents put on him to build character also created impatience — impatience with his own efforts and now impatience with his grandson's efforts. He tried to use the experts' advice, from a book which claims to tell parents how to teach a toddler to read. But, as he found, the child usually sets the agenda and Gramps must read the clues and then participate. When toddler Ronald, the expert on his own desires and powers, paid no attention to the flash cards Gramps held up, Gramps quickly learned to forego "expert" advice and his own feeling of urgency.

One of the basic questions facing grandparents and parents is whether to listen to expert advice or to go purely by instinct, listening to our inner-child-of-the-past. If we choose the latter, the results will depend to a large degree on whether our own parents did a good job. If they did, we slipped into parenting easily, like into a well-fitting glove. If our parents weren't that perfect, we may find ourself still acting out some of their imperfections, even as a grandparent. But most of us grandparents learned from experience that we need to look at the results of our actions, as John Colton did. We learned some flexibility. It's a good thing we did because the flip-side of discipline is flexibility — and some humor.

Each child's personality, strengths and weaknesses mandate that we adapt our approach to meet the needs of this unique individual. What works well on one of our children may work poorly on another. Times change with each generation and the culture, dress, diet and low-tech environment of ancestors may not be appropriate now. For example we can easily discard the male custom of wearing wigs and lace collars that was popular in England in the past. But do we discard their authoritarian approach to child rearing or the permissive approach of the past few decades? The question is, how do you know? To use trial and error concedes that we will make errors. Is there a better way? What do the experts tell us?

Theories

Ideal advice would be based on objective measures of relatively normal families. That's hard to come by. It's not that normal families represent a rarity. But expert psychologists and psychiatrists usually see mixed-up families. Much of their advice comes from what they see, the perspective of what not to do. Is that advice valid and valuable? Certainly. Benjamin Spock based a good part of his initial advice on the psychiatric theory of his day. He did not think he was advocating permissiveness. Instead he encouraged parents to accept normal built-in childhood behavior. While some of this came through as permissiveness much of it gave parents the sense of confidence that they needed, especially because so many were separated from their own parents and their advice. But as we noted in Chapter 1, theories change. The theories Spock used in his first books are now over forty years old. In 1978, thirty years after his first book, Spock wrote:

> "I myself formerly used the word permissive in a mildly approving way to indicate a relaxed kind of parental management as opposed to a more severe one. I sometimes use the word overpermissive as a label for those parental approaches which I think lead to spoiling. . . *I now dissociated myself from the word permissive* in order to make it clear that I've always been trying to help parents to avoid spoiling, and to help them to develop responsibility, self-discipline, and politeness in their children."

What this means is that parents have a right to be skeptical about child rearing advice even though it is all well-meant. Each of us can, for example, find and disagree with some of the deluge of books on child rearing. Everyone wants to tell us how to raise our children — and what we did wrong! It becomes downright amazing to read the contradictory advice given by the experts. At one extreme Richard

Farson, author of *Birthrights*, believed children should have the right to choose their own homes and design their own education and basically run their own lives. The implication is that children are wise enough to run their own lives.

Thomas Gordon's *Parent Effectiveness Training* edged toward permissiveness. On a community level, in the middle, Seattle's KidsPlace project encourages input by children and youth about neighborhood planning so it will reflect their needs as well as the needs of adults. James Dobson's *Dare to Discipline*, with it's popular authoritarian emphasis on parental firmness, represents a quite different approach to which many in the permissive camp object.

Some in child development and psychology refer to their fields as "a science." Indeed, they do try. Much of their work revolves around experiments designed to test or prove theories. However, Donald Campbell, a former President of the American Psychological Association, cautioned against accepting psychological theories or the results of relatively short term scientific investigations. The complexity of human behavior, of the human mind and emotions, opens most research findings to question. As physicians writing this book for grandparents, we are very aware of the limitations of scientific studies.

After five years many of the scientific articles in the medical journals prove erroneous, redundant or worthless. And most of these studies record physical attributes, the more easily measurable reactions of the body. Few experienced physicians rush in to be the first to use a new medicine. Instead, they wait until enough experience accumulates to more clearly demonstrate the worth and the complications of new "wonder drugs." Nothing replaces time and broad scale experience — partly because people react so differently to the same drug. The same can be said for "wonder advice." Good reason exists for being skeptical, even about the best of advice and experience, even our own.

Each of us, like John Colton, has our own long term experience from our childhood, and with our own children, to draw on and learn from. Sometimes it pays for parents and grandparents to follow their "instincts" about a particular child — the subconscious may recognize the child's needs better than the conscious part of the brain. Yet most of us learned that what worked well on one of our children did not work at all on the next. It almost makes one wonder if they really were the product of the same set of parents — if they share the same genes. Actually they don't share all of the same genes. Genetic scientists calculate, on the basis of the different amino acid building blocks of genes, that the potential exists for 64 billion unique genetic individuals. The pieces of this genetic mosaic form a baseline picture of who and what you are and how you react. What works on one person may not work on another. One man's meat is another man's poison. So research based on theories often resists generic application. But how about research based on observation?

Objective observation of different parenting methods and their effect on the children should produce the most dependable results. Neutral scientific observers, not trying to prove a theory, measure the type of parenting and record how the children turn out. But even this is not a fool-proof method. Children of the same type of parents turn out quite differently; some good, some bad. We expect some to turn out opposite to the statistical majority! However, measuring and describing those parenting methods which work best on most children helps us get at the truth. It identifies those parenting characteristics which increase the competence, confidence and social responsibility of most children. None of the results are 100%. The best type of parenting resulted in most, but not all, children becoming completely competent while the worst type of parents still produced some partially competent children. So after we choose, we should look at the results and be prepared to change if what we do doesn't seem to work.

IMPROVING OUR PARENTING STYLES

The variety of parenting styles is as great as the variety of parents, yet a logical grouping of parenting types exists. Such groupings help us understand how we parented our own children as they grew, and enables us to learn from the experiences of others who parented similarly as well as differently. Using this knowledge we can set a logical course for parenting both our adult-children and grandchildren.

Diana Baumrind conducted objective observational studies of parents at the Institute of Human Development at the University of California, Berkeley. From this she outlined five useful broad groupings of basic parenting styles. These can, perhaps, be best understood by the amount and type of power used by parents. This starts with a given: the power balance between parent and child changes with age as the child grows. Each child necessarily develops her own powers to become a successful and responsible adult. Such power manifests itself at birth — a baby's cry creates major emotional responses in Mother and Father, usually bringing out the protective parental instincts. On this basis the infant learns to trust and develops confidence in her ability to have an effect on the world. The child's power increases through the rest of the period of growth and development. How effective her personal power will be depends to a considerable degree on how she is parented.

Look at the following descriptions of parenting styles and then concentrate on those characteristics which best describe your own past methods and attitudes. Then, with this understanding, look at the results your style of parenting may have had on your adult-child. Following that, compare your style to that of the "ideal" parent, whose children turned out best, and decide whether a change in your attitude and methods will be beneficial. The five basic styles of parents, starting at the top with the worst – those whose children turn out the most poorly – are listed in order of effectiveness.

TABLE 2-1

STYLES OF PARENTING

Rejecting-Neglecting

Permissive

Authoritarian

Traditional

Rational-Authoritative

Baumrind's Thirty-Year Study

The results of short term studies often do not hold up in the long run. Long term studies take more time, more funds and more patience than most researchers and scholars have. Fortunately the time, funds and patience were found by Baumrind who recently completed her thirty year study of a fairly average group of parents and their children. Taking care not to interfere, researchers observed and carefully measured the type of parenting and the outcome of the children in terms of competence and social responsibility. These children are now relatively young adults. This one-of-a-kind study produced a cornucopia of information on which Dr. Baumrind will report in an upcoming scientific monograph. The characteristics Baumrind used to define competence are listed in Table 2-2.

TABLE 2-2

THE MOST CHARACTERISTIC FEATURES OF THE OPTIMALLY COMPETENT CHILD*

Has a sense of identity

Socially confident with adults

Interacts smoothly with other children

Comfortable and secure with adults

Willing to pursue tasks alone

Accepts responsibility for wrongdoing

Trustworthy

Will question adult authority

Persistent

Peer leader

Optimistic

Sees adults realistically

Altruistic

Internally motivated to get good grades and to learn

Argues with other children to get her/his point across

Confident of her/his intellectual abilities

Respects the work of other children

Challenges herself/himself physically

Problem oriented

Expresses negative feeling openly and directly

---

* From Love and Power/Parent and Child, Glenn Austin, M.D.,
   Robert Erdmann Publishing.

Baumrind's findings are supported by another objective study done by Professor Stanley Coopersmith who separately interviewed mothers and the teachers of their children. He compared mothering attitudes with teacher measures of student competence. Mothers whose parenting style allowed the children to help make decisions about their lives turned out to be more competent. In still another study, Burton White's Harvard Preschool Project compared mothering techniques and the development of the child's I.Q. and language in the first three years of life. Children whose mothers controlled them but allowed them to exercise their own powers, similar to the rational-authoritative mothers of Baumrind's study, developed higher than expected IQs and language ability. Using White's techniques the Department of Education of the State of Missouri sent teachers to the homes to teach young mothers this style of raising their infants and toddlers. The results of this Parents As Teachers Project were similar to those of the Harvard study.

All of these objective non-theoretical approaches produced compatible findings and helpful information for parents and grandparents. The statistical results of Baumrind's work are shown in Table 2-3. She compared Authoritarian, Traditional, Rational-Authoritative, Permissive and Rejecting-Neglecting parents. Their parenting methods can be best understood by comparing the three basic styles, Authoritarian, Rational-Authoritative and Permissive.

Comparison of Basic Styles of Parenting

Authoritarian parents overcontrol their children and do not respect them enough to let them make choices — to have the experience of making enough of their own decisions and reaping the consequences, good or bad. Their harsh discipline and overcontrol tends to suppress their children. Children learn best from the results of the choices they make and the consequences they reap. Authoritarian parents generally allow their girls more freedom of expression than the boys and, probably as a result, many of the girls develop better than the boys.

On the other end of the spectrum, objective measures show that permissive parents exert too little control and set too few limits. In the past such children had limits imposed on them in the schools and neighborhoods, but most of these social limits have decreased over the years. One result is that such children seem to have more freedom than they can handle. This makes many of them insecure. Permissive mothers were evidently poor images, for their girls did not become very competent. Some of the boys became competent anyway, possibly because they were innately talented, aggressive, and overpowered their mothers.

The children of traditional parents, a balanced team with a somewhat authoritarian father and a somewhat permissive mother, developed better than either authoritarian or permissively raised children. Most children of rejecting-neglecting parents turned out poorly, although a good number became partially competent.

Almost all of the children of rational-authoritative parents became fully competent. Their boys and girls developed equally well. We can probably learn more from these successful parents and their techniques than we can from theories or the studies of families in trouble which form the basis of so much child rearing advice. For example, one key characteristic of rational-authoritative parents is that an ideal balance of power exists between parents and their children.

TABLE 2-3

THE EFFECTS OF VARIOUS STYLES OF PARENTING

Parent Type	Competence of Their Children							
	Fully Competent		Partially Competent		Incompetent		Numbers	
	boys	girls	boys	girls	boys	girls	boys	girls
Rational-Authoritative	83%	86%	17%	14%	00%	00%	6	7
Traditional	43%	50%	57%	33%	00%	17%	14	6
Authoritarian	18%	42%	55%	58%	27%	00%	11	12
Permissive	20%	00%	69%	71%	20%	29%	5	7
Rejecting-Neglecting	00%	00%	33%	63%	67%	27%	9	8
Total							45	40

*   From Love and Power/Parent and Child, Glenn Austin, M.D.,
    Robert Erdmann Publishing.

Parenting Styles and The Use of Power

Both parent and child need and use power. The proper balance of power between the parent and the child appears to produce more competent and confident children. Unlike permissive parents, rational-authoritative parents demand good behavior and use firm discipline to control their children, but unlike authoritarian parents they balance this control with freedom for the child. The child can explore and is encouraged to stand up for himself. Equally important, while rational-authoritative parents demand respect from the child they, in turn, respect the child. *They listen to, allow or encourage the child to take the lead and the initiative. They let the child argue with them and even win on occasions if the child presents a good case. They increasingly share their power with the child, thus teaching him how to use power effectively.*

The following case composites demonstrating different styles of parenting are real. The names and circumstances are altered to protect the identity of the individuals. They show some of the traps which occur with different types of parenting and the effects on the children.

REJECTING-NEGLECTING PARENTS

We start by looking at examples of rejecting-neglecting parents who constituted around 15% of the parents in the U.C. study. We will first look at Jim, a respected police officer, who was raised by a rejecting and neglecting father and mother.

Jim

Thirty-two year old Jim, looking sharp in his neatly pressed police uniform, came in for counseling because his second marriage threatened to go sour. The problem could be traced to Jim's father, Harold, who was occupied almost solely with his career and drinking buddies and to Jim's mother who was cold and withdrawn from both her husband and her children. When Harold was home he usually ignored Jim, and if he did pay any attention to him it usually took the form of angry criticism or physical punishment. Jim was more comfortable on the streets and stayed home as little as possible. One of his more positive experiences with adults occurred when he fell under the jurisdiction of police officer Grady for shoplifting when he was 15 years old. Officer Grady took an interest in Jim, convinced him that better ways existed to get what he wanted and encouraged him to finish school and go to college. Jim went to City College where he took a law enforcement major, went on through the Police Academy and became a successful police officer himself.

Jim's upbringing led him to uncontrolled temper outbursts mimicking his father. At work he kept his temper under control and used warm professionalism, but things were different at home. His preoccupation with his career and his constant criticism and angry outbursts against his first wife led to divorce. Now with his second wife and two young children the same problems recurred. He saw too little of his family and when he did he was critical and often angry. His wife finally gave him an ultimatum: get his temper and negative attitude under control or face another divorce.

Jim really loved his family in spite of his actions. He went to his pastor who heard his problems out and, as Jim said, "opened my eyes to the way I act around Molly and the kids. I treat her and the children the same way my father treated me. I don't want to do that." On his pastor's advice he went to his pediatrician and said, "I want to learn how to be a good father. Can you help me?"

Rejected children usually remain angry at their parents and often carry this anger in them as adults. Then under stress they explode, usually taking it out on the spouse or their children. They frequently carry a feeling of worthlessness with them into adulthood because they were not valuable enough to the parents to be given the love and attention others received as children. Then they fall in love, and life suddenly seems wonderful for the adult-child who was rejected and neglected in the past. This usually leads to marriage. But when the ordinary stresses of marriage or parenthood occur, the long-retained anger left over from a loveless childhood erupts. The incidents triggering uncontrolled anger usually do not deserve anywhere near the amount of anger they release. This destroyed Jim's first marriage and was well on the way to destroying his second. The conflict created this time motivated him to seek help.

Making Up

What can you, as an older adult, do if you realize that you rejected and neglected your child, now your adult-child? The first step is to talk over your concerns with a counselor. The next step most likely would be to offer a sincere apology to your adult-child and offer your love. His need to be loved by his parents has never ceased. It may help to tell him how you were raised by your own parents, his grandparents. Most often they too were rejecting and neglecting. They really thought that a child didn't need much love and attention because that was how they were raised. Not knowing how to give love, in fact being threatened by any feeling that might draw them closer to another person, they rejected their children. Some were cruel, and whether they beat their children or not they often abused them verbally. They did not know how to give praise, appeared self-centered and often neglected the child. Yet, interestingly enough, they fed, clothed and protected their children. Not knowing how to demonstrate love doesn't mean that they didn't feel love for their children.

Such parents and grandparents still have the opportunity to learn to both give and receive love. Your love is there. It can open a new life for you if you were rejected and neglected as a child. Start by pointing out the difficulty you have had shaking the influence of your upbringing and express the hope that your son will be able to do a better job with his children than you did. State your hope that such poor parenting will not be passed on to the next generation. Don't dwell on the errors of the past after you admit them. Cry about them if you need to, then go about improving your parenting and grandparenting. Offer your love and respect even if you feel it may not be returned after the way you treated your Jim in the past. Even a little effort and a little improvement feels good.

Jim's father, Harold, started this change when he became a grandfather. He finally did succeed in re-establishing a warm and friendly relationship with Jim and his family, especially with his grandchildren, but it wasn't easy.

Harold

Harold, now a 59-year-old alcoholic, pushed his glass in circles on the polished bar and unhappily stared at his reflection on the wet surface. He fought his urge to down the whole drink in one satisfying series of gulps. He needed that drink badly after what his son had just told him over the phone, "Jim always was a snot" Harold murmured to himself angrily. Yet he recognized that Jim had told the truth. He was an alcoholic. That didn't hurt as much as being told that he was not welcome to come to his son's home and bring a present for four-year-old Joey's birthday. Jim said Joey was still frightened from Harold's last drunken visit when he hollered at Joey's mother and called her a slut because she had tried to keep him from drinking more.

Harold shook his head in dismay at the memory. Jim was right. He had made an ass of himself and really couldn't blame them for not wanting him around. His hand trembled with the urge to lift the glass of whiskey and drain it, but his heavy heart and a small inner voice fought the urge. He should go to Alcoholics Anonymous like he had promised Jim. He felt lonely and abandoned without the family. Head hanging, he looked at his reflection on the wet bar which reflected the lines on his tense face. In disgust he pushed himself away from the bar, leaving the drink untouched, and walked out determined to start with an AA counselor right away. It was time for a change. The old Asian legend says, "One step begins a long journey."

A Way Out

Above all, the best thing you can do to help your grandchildren is to face your own problems and get them under control. Go for counseling or psychiatric help. Rein in your temper. Join Alcoholics Anonymous if you drink too much. Grow up. By doing so you will offer your children and grandchildren an inspiring model of courage and determination not to let life or your problems get you down. Do this for yourself and for your grandchildren. Set an example!

Although most of us do not fit the above descriptions we have all made mistakes. We can overcome these mistakes because the experience and the maturity which comes with age helps us to face our past, learn from it, and do a better job now and in the future. Even if you were a rejecting or neglecting parent your children still haven't outgrown their need for your love. Even some physically abused children, given the choice, will return to their abusing parents. After all, their parents gave them life, fed them, housed and clothed them. As bad as they may be, parents still can represent security. Children have to love their parents or they feel guilty and insecure for hating them. They want to love you. Give them a chance.

How can you start building a positive relationship with your adult-children? Start by not blaming them, a tendency many parents have when they don't get along with their children. Face up to your own imperfections. Start now learning how to parent better and how to be an effective loving parent and grandparent. Study the model of the rational-authoritative parent in this and the following chapters which may help you improve your parenting skills. This will help you become a sensible grandparent. The rewards can be great, starting with the basic knowledge that "I really tried!" Then you will feel better about yourself and experience far better relationships with your family.

Permissive Parents

The difference between rejecting-neglecting and permissive parenting probably represents the degree of parental love. Permissive parents love their children so much that they seem unable to say no to them or to establish boundaries. They shower their children with gifts, give them excessive attention and reward them with unearned respect. Their children develop high opinions of themselves, often undeserved, yet they are anxious about the lack of limits and structure in their lives. Children instinctively look for limits and structure. Without externally imposed limits to control their behavior they feel insecure. Never having to earn approval by producing adult behavior, they see little need to mature or take responsibility for their actions. This is what Irene, an attractive grandmother ready to retire from her job as secretary, told us had happened to her daughter Sue:

Sue

Thirty-one-year old Sue called her mother on the telephone to complain about her third husband's behavior. "Jerry's impossible Mom. He expects me to keep the house clean, get his dinner, balance the checkbook, and take care of Jeanne and now he wants another baby! I'd like to see him home all day with a two-year-old as active as Jeanne. Yesterday she broke that pretty crystal lamp the Voughts gave us for a wedding gift. She just won't leave things alone. I don't know how you raised two of us! I told Jerry, no way am I going to have another baby."

Sue, a sparkling attractive brunette with a confident air, had almost the same complaints about her first two husbands. She had had an affair with Wes while married to her first husband, leading to her first divorce and marriage to Wes. But although she enjoyed Wes and even told her mother that they had great sex together and she felt loved, she felt that he didn't make enough money. While Irene was still charmed by her delightful but "flaky" daughter, after listening to her complaints about all the men in her life, one after another, she began to wonder if Sue had a responsible bone in her body. Irene's husband, Sue's dad, earned less than Wes did. Irene remembered the blow up when Wes came home to find that Sue had bought a new sports car without his knowledge. This, added to all her past credit card purchases put them into an impossible financial situation. Sue had sulked when he forced her to take the car back, at a considerable loss. This soon led to the second divorce even though her mother had given Sue several thousand dollars to help her out of the financial crisis she had created.

Irene sighed, listening to Sue ramble on about what she considered Jerry's inconsiderate behavior. Sue complained that she didn't have time to lunch at the Country Club much any more nor to go to her exercise class. "Baby sitters are hard to get anymore," she complained, "and they always want to know exactly when I will come back. As if I were on their schedule!" she huffed. Irene, now the grandmother of that delightful but spoiled preschool girl of Sue's, had more to think about than keeping Sue happy. Sue didn't talk much about her baby and sometimes seemed to resent her husband or her mother giving attention to Jeanne. Sue might be 31-years-old but she still acted like a spoiled child. She never seemed to accept her responsibilities, never seemed to see that she created most of her own problems. While Sue was charming and fun to be around, the selfishness and constant complaining about how people treated her was bothersome.

Sue badly needed to grow up, to act more like a mother than a teenager. Even though she dearly loved two-year-old Jeanne she came perilously close to neglecting her because of her country clubbing, shopping and beauty parlor time. Baby sitters avoided working for her because they couldn't depend on her coming back when she said she would. And one day-care refused to take Jeanne because Sue was so involved in an afternoon cocktail party that the time "just slipped away" and she didn't pick Jeanne up until around eight-thirty that evening.

Sue's increasing complaints about her problems, her self-absorption and her neglect of her child indicated a real need for help. Once the apple of mother's eye, Irene now recognized that she had given Sue too much and expected too little. She had been a permissive parent. Sue hadn't really grown up, nor did she take responsibility for her life or for Jeanne. Irene couldn't let Jeanne be neglected — her granddaughter deserved better than that.

Making Up

Irene realized that she had been too permissive when she raised Sue. This realization was the first step in trying to correct the situation. Her next step is to learn how to develop good parenting skills and put them to practice on her adult-child. For this to be effective, she will have to explain to Sue that her permissive child raising had not served Sue well and that both she and Sue need education on how to break out of the poor habits of the past.

Authoritarian Parents

Authoritarian Parenting produces more competent and socially responsible children than permissive parenting. However, the boys of authoritarian parents turned out very poorly in Baumrind's study. Authoritarian parents are rigid and they especially overcontrol their boys. Looking at parenting from a historical and evolutionary perspective it is not hard to understand why so many parents used authoritarian methods. Throughout history, civilization and structure was often kept intact by harsh authority. Feudal lords ruled with an iron hand. Churches, whether Christian, Jewish or Mohammedan generally had an authoritarian structure and rigid rules of conduct. Employers were harsh, demanding and occasionally capricious. Authoritarianism of various dictatorships, be they the pure arbitrary use of power by Central American strong men or the ideological rationalizations of communism, still plagued society during the last half of the 20th century. Immigrants from Europe and Asia brought a long history of rigid family structure with them from the old country. Many of today's grandparents grew up in an atmosphere of authoritarianism.

Authoritarian child rearing is not all bad. The rigid rules prevented many children from getting into trouble. Rigid family structure offers security and a sense of belonging. The demand for good behavior often produced responsible children. In Baumrind's study, most of the boys and all of the girls grew up partially competent or better. But many of the boys became incompetent and many who were partially competent have problems, like Mike, traceable to their harsh authoritarian upbringing.

Mike

Mike brushed away the sweat dripping from his forehead as he put the telephone down. He felt relieved that he had an appointment with his old pediatrician but his stomach still churned when he looked at his wife Lori, rocking their toddler. Mary still sobbed from her fright when Mike angrily hollered at her and shook his fist after she had pulled over and spilled the garbage pail. He had been close to hitting her and the 200 pounds behind his fist could have seriously injured her. Lori, blond hair flying and blue eyes snapping, had pulled Mike away and led him to their bedroom when he balled his fist. In her calm but authoritative voice with an edge of hardness to it, she had said, "Mike, stop that bellowing this instant. You've scared Mary to death! Now I've told you before that you had better call Dr. Brown. Lets go see if he can help you get that temper under control. This time does it. Either you call or Mary and I are leaving you. You call — now!"

Mike put up the phone, hung his head and said, "God, I'm sorry. I keep acting like my folks did whenever I did anything wrong. Dr. Brown warned us that I might have trouble controlling myself when we had a child. I hate myself! Honey, I'm sorry. We have an appointment Saturday and I'll put off that wiring job."

When Lori was pregnant Mike had proudly taken her to meet his old pediatrician. Now a hard working electrician, he still looked on Dr. Brown fondly, remembering the times as a teenager when the doctor had calmed down the family squabbles and sometimes by calm reasoning convinced his folks to punish him less. They had punished him a lot. Once he carried a bruise on his neck for a couple of weeks when his dad had hit him for talking back. When Mike graduated from high school and was leaving home he had visited Dr. Brown to say good by. Dr. Brown had encouraged him to leave as soon as he graduated to get away from his folks' anger. He explained to Mike that his folks did love him but that they had both been raised by punitive parents and almost instinctively overreacted to anything Mike did. Earlier he had told Mike's folks to stop the physical punishment and cool it or he would have to call the authorities. Mike remembered the shock on his father's face and his angry scowl as he rasped out in reply, "But I have to punish him! His grades are awful and he keeps trying to talk back."

Mike had kept quiet in the corner as Dr. Brown calmly said, "Look Bill, I know you feel that you are doing the right thing. But Mike is afraid of you. Is that what you want from your child? Fear? You do love him, so show it by controlling yourself. You can't beat or browbeat a boy into really doing well in school. He has to want to himself."

After that Mike's dad didn't hit him but his mother acted even more angry over little things. When Mike said his good by to Dr. Brown, the doctor took advantage of the visit to tell him that when he had children of his own he might find himself acting just like his folks did — and that he should learn to control himself. Mike recalled that warning. Now the warning was coming to pass. Mike found himself frustrated on his job and angry at his boss. When he came home the littlest thing would set him off. Luckily Lori was usually able to cope and calm him down. Now she demanded that he change.

Mike's outbursts didn't make him feel any better about himself. His lack of confidence and underlying anger at authority figures made it difficult for him to get along with his boss. He kept control on the job because he had to, but at home he blew up more and more. Such behavior is typical of an adult-child raised by exceptionally harsh authoritarian parents. His lack of confidence, rebellion against authority and inability to stand up to an over-demanding boss created stresses he could only take out at home. Luckily his wife would not put up with it. After she had Mike go see Dr. Brown she took it upon herself to tell Mike's parents that she needed their help — that the feelings of worthlessness and anger they left in Mike needed to be replaced with acceptance and love.

Mike's folks were still not used to having someone tell them that they had done a poor job raising their son. But they remembered

Dr. Brown's warnings and were aware that Mike avoided them whenever he could. That especially hurt because they loved Mike and loved
their granddaughter. Their anger, hurt and guilt were stirred up when
Lori calmly but determinedly confronted them, "Look, Mom and Dad,
we have a problem. Mike is having trouble getting along with his boss
and he has been losing his temper around Mary. You remember Dr.
Brown telling you that you were too harsh on him. Well, I had Mike go
see Dr. Brown again after he almost hit Mary with his fist and Dr. Brown
suggested that I talk with you. He advised that we all read some books
on new findings about the results of authoritarian parenting and
maybe even take a class on parenting at Evergreen Junior College."

Then, before she left for home, Lori smiled and said, "Mike
and I were wondering if you would like to go on vacation with us this
summer. We thought we'd camp at Lone Pine Lake. And Mary will be
in heaven if her grandma and grandpa could come play with her." This
defused their anger and defensiveness, made them recognize that they
were wanted and accepted. It made it far easier for them to try to
change and help Mike.

Grandparents who were harsh and rigid with their children
often find that their adult-children avoid them, making it difficult to
see their grandchildren. They also find that the grandchildren sometimes get away with murder because they are raised permissively. This
often represents their adult-child's reaction against the way he was
raised and is especially galling to grandparents who did their best to
raise their children right and believe in strict discipline.

Ways Out

Parents who have been too authoritarian in the past usually
mellow with age. Recognition of the need of the now adult-child to
run his own family and make his own decisions usually helps avoid
friction. Admitting that you were too controlling and that you have
learned better ways to deal with people, especially your children and
grandchildren, helps. A frank discussion of the virtue and amount of
control and structure required to keep kids out of trouble, balanced

with the need for self-expression and personal decision making, may help you and your adult-child take a more rational look at the needs of your grandchildren.

Traditional Parenting

Traditional parents balance each other. Usually Mother is a bit more permissive and nurturing and Dad demands more and uses firmer discipline. In Baumrind's U.C. study group all of the boys of traditional parents and most of the girls were partially or fully competent. When serious problems are seen in clinical practice in traditional families they frequently spring from the lack of a team approach.

Courting couples rarely ask each other what sort of parents each will be. If they did they probably wouldn't know, even if they thought they knew. Parenting brings out the instinctive feelings and imprints of the past. How we were raised and reacted to our childhood experiences combines with our genetic personalities to subconsciously direct our parenting from an emotional level. We do what "feels" right. If both parents have reasonably similar backgrounds a team approach is relatively easy. If they don't, if father reacts to his child's misbehavior in an angry authoritarian manner while mother's background and reaction is the permissive opposite, then the fat's in the fire. When father punishes, mother protests. This makes father angrier and he punishes harder to compensate for what he sees as mother's spoiling.

Children instinctively seize the opportunity to play one parent against the other. Commonly this results in a "good guy" mother and a "bad guy" father in the eyes of the child. A warring triangle evolves in which the child exerts his power by behaving in a way which he knows will drive dad up the wall. The extent of the problems and the variations of this theme create continuing conflict. This conflict can last a lifetime unless a new approach is taken, as Robert, a traditional parent found when he became a grandfather.

Robert

Robert, now a graying grandfather, went to a psychologist to ask how he could get closer to his daughter Ann and his grandson. Ann wouldn't invite him over and when he did come, her coldness drove him out. Robert was also concerned about Ann's drug use and drinking. This wasn't new. Ann, now twenty-five-years old, had always seemed to hate her dad. He remembered arguing with his wife, Marcella, about discipline back when Ann was five-years-old, often in front of the child. Ann's mother let her do almost anything she wanted and seemed to take delight in thwarting his attempts to discipline or control her.

Robert clearly remembered the time when he had positive proof that his wife tried to make him look like the bad guy in Ann's eyes. Ann, then fourteen-years old, asked her Mother for permission to go to a punk rock concert. Mother said that she would discuss it with Dad. She did, and they both agreed that the drug exposure was too great to permit her to go. But Mother's attitude seemed peculiar so when she went upstairs to Ann's room to tell her, Dad hesitated a minute and then decided to also go. As he approached Ann's bedroom door he heard his wife say, "Well Honey, you can't go. I tried to talk your dad into letting you go but you know how he is." Since that time Robert felt alienated from his wife although he stayed married.

The psychologist pointed out that Ann had a lifetime of learning to hate Father and that such a problem would not be easily resolved. The psychologist spent time with Robert's wife and gradually learned that she had hated her own father because she thought him too strict, and she decided to protect Ann from what she perceived as excess strictness from Robert. She defended her permissiveness half-heartedly because she was also worried and felt guilty about Ann's drug use. She tried to blame Robert's strictness for Ann's behavior, but the psychologist concentrated on how she had reacted to her own father and the fact that she still seemed to be genuinely in love with Robert. He gave her enough insight that she finally realized that she had unjustly colored her behavior towards Robert because of her reaction to her own father, when in fact Robert was not very authoritarian. She was then able to start the long road to rehabilitate Robert in their daughter's eyes.

RATIONAL-AUTHORITATIVE PARENTS

Parents aren't perfect. But some parents do a better job than others as measured by the outcome of the children. Looking at successful models allows all types of grandparents and parents to learn how to improve their own parenting. Grandparents do parent their adult-children. Parenting is forever. Can grandparents learn enough from the experience of rational-authoritative parents to help them function more effectively? Certainly major differences exist between a parent's role and responsibility while the child grows and after the child becomes an adult.

Good parenting should result in the children becoming competent, confident and socially responsible adults. Baumrind's thirty years of objective measurements of the way parents raised their children and the effects on the children, demonstrated that rational-authoritative parents were the most effective. These parents balanced their firm structure and control, their consistent demand for responsible behavior, with affection and respect. By giving the child increasing freedom to be responsible for his own actions and opportunities to develop his own initiative, rational-authoritative parents helped their children feel capable and confident. In discipline they tended to let the child's problems be his own so the parent's control was exerted firmly but neutrally, not with anger or criticism. Thus the child felt that he made a lot of decisions about his own life and learned to accept the consequences. He was guided by strong adults who used their power to teach him the rewards and punishments which followed his decisions.

Because rational-authoritative parenting is the method we can learn from best and will examine most closely, we will concentrate on it in the next three chapters. As you will see, grandparents often naturally begin to use this style when they become sensible grandparents.

THE GRANDPARENT'S ADVANTAGE

A significant percentage of parents are rational and authoritative. It becomes exciting to look at what happens to the majority of parents as they learn from experience over the years. With age and wisdom burnished by the successes and failures which occurred in raising their children, most grandparents have become more rational and authoritative. They are more sensible. Grandparents naturally modify and improve their past methods when dealing with their adult-children and grandchildren. In the following chapters we will share some of their experiences and then describe sensible grandparenting and look at how it effects the way they parent their adult-children.

3   SENSIBLE GRANDPARENTING
Learning From Experience

What most grandparents learned, without the benefit of books or experts, generally turns out to be compatible with rational-authoritative parenting methods. We will call this Sensible Grandparenting. Such methods come more easily to grandparents than they did while they were raising their own children. First, most grandparents have developed better self control than they had when they were raising their own children. They have usually learned to appreciate the power needs of children. At the same time they discover that they have a very powerful effect on their grandchildren, especially as they develop the ability to control them diplomatically. This control starts with the grandparent's attention which offers the children the reward of respect as well as fun and security.

Grandparents rarely need to punish by scolding, isolation or spanking. That's the parent's domain. Grandparents usually control by rationally withdrawing their attention and their rewards, if the child misbehaves. The rewards are privileges, not rights. On top of that children generally hold their grandparents in some awe. The awe, respect, enjoyment, admiration and curiosity about their roots often combines to motivate kids to behave better for their grandparents than they do for their parents. If they don't behave properly the rewards are simply withdrawn. Scolding, isolation or spanking are rarely needed unless the grandparent functions as an almost full-time parent. Even then, the neutral discipline technique of making the child's problems his instead of yours comes naturally to grandparents. Of the three generations, child/parent/grandparent, the relations between the skip-generations of grandparent to grandchild produce fewer power struggles than between parent and child.

TABLE 3-1

**SUMMARY OF SENSIBLE GRANDPARENTING
METHODS**

1. Reward your grandchild with the privilege of attention, play and respect.

2. Through story telling offer models which show children how to behave in a productive and socially responsible manner.

3. Demand good behavior.

4. If the child doesn't behave properly, withdraw your attention.

5. Offer opportunities to start fresh at a later time.

6. Bite your tongue and let the parents do the active discipline unless you are directly responsible for the child.

7. When you can, get the child alone with you so he will have fewer distractions and you can have more effective control.

HOW WE LEARNED

Most of us started parenting by the seat of our pants, using our own parents' imprint, but we found that experience is a great teacher. Some of the ways we handled our children, that felt right for us, didn't work all that well. Even if it worked well on one of our children it didn't necessarily work well on others. So we changed, and most grandparents have already improved their parenting skills to a significant degree. This improvement needn't stop, and your reading this book says it hasn't for you. You join those of us who know that it is never too late to learn. Few of us were perfect parents and we each made our share of mistakes. So now that we face grandparenting we would like to do a better job. Not only that, parenting really goes on forever, a part of lifelong learning. We even still have an opportunity to improve the parenting of our adult-children. Here we will discuss a few of the more common traps which can interfere with sensible parenting and grandparenting. Our maturity allows us to learn, to change attitudes and improve our skills without being defensive. We learn from the mistakes that we and others have made. One of the most common mistakes is punishment by guilt.

EXPERIENCE: GUILT

Punishment by guilt has been a way of life for many parents and some are astonished to be told to use it sparingly if at all. But, as you will see, good reasons exist to generally avoid guilt-producing sorrow or anger in dealing with your adult children or grandchildren. Some use guilt consciously by telling a child, "You make me feel bad." The hurt look on a mother's face induces guilt. Many parents use guilt in more sophisticated ways. In the syndicated comic strip "Cathy," Cathy's mother uses guilt in such outrageous quantities and ways to hold her daughter to her that we are forced to laugh. That sort of manipulation by guilt is a natural part of human behavior. But how productive guilt techniques are is open to question. Battles may be won but causes lost.

Most guilt feelings in children result from parental or grand-parental anger. Anger punishes in many ways. First it takes away love, it threatens. Parental anger says that the child is bad, perhaps worthless. Displeasing the parent enough to make him or her angry may make the child feel he will be abandoned. Most of all, parental anger creates guilt, and guilt leads to many reactions. The punishment of guilt is heavy enough that it usually forces the child to obey. Occasionally its use may be deserved. But it usually creates resentment, even an underlying desire to get even. It diminishes self-esteem. And it lasts. There are better ways of handling problems:

Johnny

Four-year-old Johnny took two-year-old Jeremy's Ninja Turtle from him, hit him and pushed him away when he tried to grab it back. Mother heard Jeremy scream — it had been a long day and she was tired of the boys fighting all the time. This time did it! Her anger boiled over and she came into the room red-faced and hollering at Johnny, "What did you do this time! I told you not to hit your little brother. What am I going to do with you? If you hit him once more I'm going to spank you until you can't sit down for a week!"

Johnny paled, gulped and quickly handed the Ninja Turtle back to his little brother. He was frightened, both by his mother's anger and her threat. His stomach churned and he felt like vomiting. He was real mad at Jeremy and thought, "Mother loves him and hates me!" He blinked back his tears and went over and threw himself face down on his bed.

Had Grandmother been there instead of mother she would have walked into the room calmly and said, "Well, what's all the fuss about? Oh, I see. Isn't that Jeremy's Ninja Turtle you have Johnny?" Johnny whined, "But, he had it all day. And he broke mine Grandma. So I took his!"

Grandmother would nod, murmuring, "Hum. . ." and then say, "Well, it's good to share but it's not good to take things. You didn't like it when Jeremy took your Ninja and broke it, did you? Uh huh. Well you're the big brother and you don't want to act like a little two-year-old like Jeremy, do you? Why don't you show him how a good big brother should act and give him back his turtle. When he gets older he will appreciate how you taught him to behave like a big boy instead of like a baby."

If Johnny refuses, then Grandmother calmly says, "Johnny, give that back to Jeremy now. If you don't I guess it is because you must be really tired. Otherwise you wouldn't act like a two-year-old yourself. You must be too tired for a bedtime story tonight — I guess we had better put you to bed a little earlier than usual so you can get your rest."

This way the problem remains Johnny's and the solution, the reward or punishment for his behavior, is up to him. If he has to be punished by going to bed earlier than usual then he paid for his misbehavior. It doesn't leave him feeling unloved or really bad. It leaves him wondering if it was worth it to take the toy from Jeremy and starts the development of conscience without a feeling of guilt.

Guilt represents the most severe punishment parents can use on children. It leaves many children in a panic, fearful that they will be abandoned and are no longer loved, or worth loving. After an episode of parental anger, the child will frequently come to the parent and offer a timid, "I love you mommy." Other children react with counter anger and continue to misbehave to punish their parents in return. They still feel bad, but their instinctive pride and competitiveness make them fight. It spawns runaways. The sad part about the outcome is that the guilt feelings tend to last, often forever. They can remain a source of strain between a parent and the adult-child.

Some psychologists believe that guilt offers the best way to teach a child, a sure way to internalize good behavior and thus develop a conscience. Conscience becomes the warning, the internal sense of right and wrong. But psychiatrists recognize that guilt creates more than conscience, it creates fear of abandonment and an inner compulsion to be punished. By being punished one atones for the bad behavior and thus relieves the guilt. Such feelings are not uncommon in childhood. Most of us remember the child who deliberately acted up in a way that he knew would result in punishment. After the spanking the child seemed relieved and happy. It was a sort of quid pro quo, "I got mad and hurt your feelings Mom, and then you hurt me. Now we are even and can start over." However, conscience based on guilt results in background feelings of fear and anxiety. Some of us still have some of these feelings remaining as part of our inner child of the past, that subconscious part of our being which often directs what we do.

Guilt is a powerful tool to control children of any age. And certainly children need control and must develop a conscience. But, as we will see, conscience can be developed in most children in a less damaging way. As grandparents looking back, many of us recognize that logic, love and action taught the same lesson and internalized good behavior without the hurt of guilt.

Good Grandparenting and Conscience

Conscience develops as a result of the teaching of rational parents and sensible grandparents. First, the rational parent teaches by being a model. If we want our children not to hurt people, we don't hurt people ourselves when we can avoid it. Second, we demand good behavior. The consequences of good and bad behavior are rationally explained to the child and then reasonable consequences are enforced. As in Gilbert and Sullivan's operetta, The Mikado, "Let the punishment fit the crime!" The child has a choice and learns from the consequences of that choice. Lessons from a non-angry parent or grandparent who insists that the child behave correctly tend to last with less pain and guilt. If the child made the wrong choice, he was punished and he learned. His punishment absolved the guilt. He was left with an internalized lesson, a conscience which warns him that some temptations lead to bad results. We can learn about the mechanisms of anger, guilt and conscience and then use logic to find better ways to handle our children and grandchildren. But our instincts and the experiences recorded by our inner-child-of-the-past may make it difficult to act logically.

Logic is easier to use when we grow older for we develop an increased ability to be reflective. We can look more objectively at what we do, and then act from logic rather than impulse. Rational actions produce the best results. We can become effective, sensible grandparents — especially if we each learn to control our personal inner-child-of-the-past and avoid the trap of power struggles.

Teaching Without a Power Struggle

In teaching a grandchild, start with a low key but determined demand for good behavior. Logically and warmly explain the reasons for the demand, let him know what behavior you value and what misbehavior you will not tolerate. Sometimes this can be done indirectly. For example, Grandfather can look for the appropriate time to relate an experience:

> "That reminds me of a fellow I knew when I was in college. We were assigned to the same dormitory room. He was nice enough but he really had the manners of a pig. He left his clothes on the floor. Never swept out or cleaned up the mess he made in the bathroom. And he kept interrupting when I tried to study in the room. So I just arranged to switch rooms. You know, that guy was sloppy in his work too, and I think they booted him out of college. At least I didn't see him after that semester. Didn't miss him either!"

Grandfather expressed his values, his demands and the consequences in story form. If thirteen-year-old Johnny was sloppy and left messes in Grandfather's car when they went to the movie, then relating this story indirectly lets Johnny know where Gramps stands. The next day Johnny can be invited to help Gramps clean up his car. If he refuses, saying he is going over to a friend's house, Gramps might note that some of the mess in the car is Johnny's and say calmly with a smile, "Johnny, help me clean my car. If I have to clean it up alone every time after you are in it I doubt if I will want to take you out very much. Anyway, I enjoy having you work with me. You are fun. Let's get the job done, it won't take long and after I can give you a ride to your friend's house. When you get older maybe I can teach you to drive. By the way, do you know how the clutch works? I may have to have mine replaced."

Avoiding a power struggle, Gramps still lets Johnny know that he expects fewer messes and wants help in cleaning up those Johnny makes. If Johnny goes off without helping, the next time he asks Gramps for a ride, Gramps can say, "Gosh Johnny. I just cleaned the car. I'll give you a ride if you promise not to mess it up. O.K.? Lets go." Then no lectures, instead follow Johnny's lead and converse with him about what he seems to want to talk about. Nothing's wrong with a comfortable silence. If Johnny dumps the candy wrapper on the floor again, calmly ask him to take it out with him and put it in the garbage. If he won't, or forgets, then just refuse to take him when he asks again. Factually say, "No Johnny. You leave messes in my car and leave the cleaning to me. Doesn't seem fair, does it? You know how I am about messes. Never could tolerate messy people. Now if you will help me wash the car tomorrow — I guess I can take you. But I want a promise. What do you say?"

Johnny might be upset and refuse to help and refuse to go. But that's his problem. If Gramps sticks to his word and refuses to take Johnny anywhere if Johnny doesn't live up to his promise, then several lessons may be learned. Perhaps the most important is that Gramps is a man of his word. He says what he means and does as he says. If he doesn't scold Johnny or act upset and angry, it is less likely to interrupt their relationship. That, though, is left up to Johnny. The door is open. Gramps can start a conversation directed toward something else, away from Johnny's problem with messiness. He might ask if Johnny wants to play some Poker or do a little batting practice. Refusing to take Johnny for a ride doesn't, as far as Gramps is concerned, mean he is angry. The door is left open and no guilt trip is laid on Johnny. It's just that he can't be messy when he rides with Gramps. So it is Johnny's problem, not Gramps', and this helps build Johnny's conscience.

Listening and Winning

Another step in sensible grandparenting involves really listening to Johnny and letting him know that you are interested in what he says. Respect his opinion and even if you don't agree, tell him he made a really good argument. Allow that he might become a lawyer. Say, "You almost convinced me in spite of the fact that I know you are wrong." This builds Johnny's confidence and self-esteem even if he is wrong. If Johnny is partially right, next time you see him say, "Johnny, I looked up that book on baseball we were talking about and you know, you were right about the date. But it was Lou Gehrig who made the most valuable player of the year that year."

Few things in life are clear cut. It never hurts to admit that we have been wrong. Rigidity isn't necessary and is rarely desirable. Consistency and flexibility are both necessary and desirable. Johnny will learn your values and may mimic them later. Grandparents make a powerful impact and the results can last a lifetime. For some children, grandparents are their only beacon, their only strong dependable model. And even if you aren't the only one offering him values, you do have an effect.

Rational parents and sensible grandparents tend to take an overall *logical* look at how they can best handle the child. They decide what they want to accomplish and make a mental list of how they will go about it. For example, if you want to teach your grandchild a sense of responsibility you can study and use the list in Table 3-2.

Table 3-2
HOW TO HELP YOUR GRANDCHILD DEVELOP
A SENSE OF RESPONSIBILITY

1. Offer a good example by helping others, completing tasks, living your good values, being honest and trustworthy, following good leaders and leading good followers.

2. Expose him to others who behave admirably and responsibility.

3. Demand good behavior. Establish and consistently enforce rules of good behavior. Contract with him and give rewards for good behavior, but withhold rewards for bad behavior.

4. When he is in your care, control your grandchild's behavior by consistent neutral discipline, making both his good and bad behavior his problem, not yours.

5. Establish repetitive habits of good behavior by consistent rational control and firmness. This gives him experience in acting properly which tends to become ingrained, assuring future habitual good behavior.

6. Offer the child a positive image of herself. Use praise. Tell her that she is a responsible and trustworthy person and point out the innate reward of respect she will receive by behaving accordingly.

7. Insist that he help with necessary household chores without any more pay than anyone else at your house receives for similar services. This shows respect for him and allows him a sense of belonging.

8. Let him share in the planning and outcome of decisions that affect him. Start with minor choices when he is young and as he matures increase his voice in major decisions.

9. Encourage him to complete his tasks by giving the contracted reward for his services only when the task is completed.

THE TRAP OF THE TRIANGLE

Often the first shock we experienced as a parent was discovering that our spouse had quite different attitudes about child rearing than we did. This sometimes initially surfaces in how parents respond to the new baby's cry. Or it may first become apparent when the exploring toddler starts getting into everything and obviously needs control. If the parents, even in the traditional family, are too far apart in their style of parenting, problems can occur. For example: Father demands a lot while Mother is very protective. If Father then punishes the child it upsets Mother, who objects that he is too harsh. This angers Father who in retaliation feels Mother is spoiling the child and therefore tries to make up for what he sees as a deficiency and comes down even harder on the child. This in turn angers Mother and starts an ongoing fight over how to raise the child. Often the fight is hidden and not verbalized, leading to chronic tension between the parents.

The child quickly picks up on the differences in attitude and style of his parents, whether they fight openly or not. Being natural manipulators, children soon learn to play one parent against the other. Some find that they have the power to "get even" with the more demanding parent by repeating the misbehavior that evoked the parent's anger to start with. This angers the parent who punishes again.

The child may accept the punishment, regarding it as a sign of victory; he knows he got even because it angered the parent. Thus the angry punishment teaches the child just the opposite of what the parent wants to teach. Repeated misbehavior often indicates that the parent, inadvertently, is rewarding that misbehavior by getting angry. This soon leads to a situation where Mother tries to protect the child, and she and the child become a team against Father.

Typical triangles are Mother and Son against Father or Father and Daughter against Mother. If Mother is the "bad guy" in the eyes of the daughter and Father is the "good guy", this Father-Daughter alliance usually lasts until early adolescence. However, by that time the daughter's hormones begin to flow and vague sexual feelings begin to stir. Father may have been the prime love of the girl until now, but suddenly the anti-incest instincts threaten this relationship. Neither really recognizes the source of the sudden discomfort, but both usually begin to give each other more space. If the team is a boy and his mother, he finds more reason not to have her hug him as she used to. These feelings add to the essential need of the adolescent to separate and establish his independence, his autonomy. This leaves the adolescent without any one to turn to for the other parent is already the bad guy and the good guy parent becomes unacceptable because of these vague feelings for a need to separate.

Grandparents are, of course, less threatening and often become the major acceptable source of adult support for the adolescent. By being aware of the potential problems that marked differences in parental discipline can create, grandparents may be able to diplomatically help the parents understand the need for teamwork. But if a grandparent offers unasked-for advice it may be resented by one or both parents. In the following chapters you will see how a grandmother helped her daughter, Sue, avoid this problem with five-year-old Jessica. You will also read how a team of grandparents helped rebellious Steve when he was an adolescent. Later you will read how a family struggle between the Father-Daughter team against Mother surfaced when Marisa and her daughter Becky moved in with her folks. Grandparents can often help defuse such situations by understanding and being available. If asked they can, as you will see, diplomatically call attention to the child's tendency to play the parents apart, and thus help the parents become a team.

GRANDPARENTS AS TEACHERS

Grandparents teach by just "being there" as a model, as a link to the past and as concrete evidence of the support within the extended family. They learn from the way we act, the stories we tell and the attitudes we project. While a function is served just by their presence, most grandparents have the potential to grandparent actively. Active involvement is needed, for these children will soon be the adults of the future and they need all of the competence and social responsibility they can muster. Recognizing this, many grandparents take pride in teaching their grandchildren.

Jesse and Gramps

Young Jesse eagerly put down his Boy Scout Handbook and made a bee line for the woodpile in the back yard, stopping only long enough in the kitchen to get a box of matches. A brand new Tenderfoot Scout, he had just hurriedly skimmed over the exciting instructions on how to build a campfire. However the twigs he gathered were too green to catch fire. Gramps stood quietly on the porch watching and waiting for the frustration to appear. When it did, and Jesse glanced up at him quizzically, he quietly offered:

"Jesse, most of us use really dry wood to start fires. Green twigs are too wet and heavy and don't catch fire very well. See how they bend? Dry twigs snap when you try to bend them and they weigh less than green twigs. Here, I'll lend you my pocket knife and you can shave some wood off one of those dry boards by the shed."

Gramps showed him how to make wood shavings and coached him in the proper way to make a fire. Jesse said little but he was obviously pleased when his fire burned brightly. Gramps showed him how to put the fire out "to keep from setting forest fires." Most importantly, Gramps let Jesse try first on his own, and only offered help when Jesse indicated that he could use help. Jesse not only received help in fire building, he received the respect of his elder. He subconsciously stored and modeled some of his behavior after Gramps and began to assimilate his values. All from the first campfire. And grandparents who give such lessons feel a deep sense of satisfaction — even if they see only the tip of the iceberg. The warmth from such a campfire lasts a lifetime.

Teaching and Having Fun

Grandparenting tends to bring out the child in us. Hopefully, we never outgrow the joy of spontaneous play. And as elders most of us have learned the value of relaxing, letting our hair down. Grandchildren teach us how to loosen up. We may even take pleasure in simple games. Chicago radio hostess Hope Daniels had fun with her six-year-old godson Brian. She wrote, "Well, this summer I visited my family and spent some time with Brian. He was excited because he has a set of checkers and his Mom had been teaching him how to play. . . and he was ready to take me on! We set up the board on the living room floor. The first game went by quickly — I beat him in a matter of minutes. Brian wasn't dismayed and we started another game. I told him how certain moves would mean he would lose and he did. But lo and behold he almost beat me on the next game — I was saved by his Mom calling him for his evening bath. As he left the room he said, 'Wait till the next visit — then I'll beat you!"

Grandparents usually feel less responsible than the parents and thus feel less guilty if the child doesn't do well. So usually they make fewer direct demands which reduces the pressure and allows the child to relax with the grandparent. For the first time some kids may feel really comfortable with an adult. Often they open a secret side to their grandparent and share unsuspected ambitions, fears or interests. Because they don't have to accept an adult power demand to produce or "be good," and don't expect punishment, they can produce and be good because they want to. They have a chance to really use their initiative. They can be natural — and naturally most kids are fun.

Grandmother Judy Hovey cautions:

"I've often heard it said that grandparenting is special, since you have the joy without the responsibility. Not so! Surely there is joy in sharing their lives, but also with it goes responsibility — to be a good example, to be a good listener when needed, resisting the temptation to be overly permissive, and to keep the lines of communication open at all times."

The other side of having fun is that grandparents normally use neutral discipline — they almost automatically parent in a sensible manner unhampered by parental guilt and anxiety. You have read about rational-authoritative parenting and neutral discipline and will read about some of the ways grandparents use these techniques at different ages in the next chapters. This style of parenting is far more fun than other styles for grandparents, parents and also for the children. It allows us to teach and control with less hassle. If the child behaves in a productive manner she has fun with Grandma. If the child misbehaves the fun stops and Grandma calmly withdraws. Thus the child's behavior is the child's problem and not the grandparents'. Neutral discipline helps the child develop self-control and a sense of responsibility for her actions.

Being around grandchildren isn't always fun, but grandchildren still want us. Oh sure, there are times when they may selfishly ignore us. Some from temperament and some from environment, may not be the loving, accepting, obedient type of grandchildren we want. But we have been around long enough to recognize that this too shall change. As people grow they evolve. Stages of negativism and selfishness often pass — are outgrown with experience. Lack of appreciation today does not mean we won't be appreciated in the future. Just as we have become wiser with age, so will they. Just as we learn that selfishness doesn't lead to happiness, so will they.

4 SENSIBLE GRANDPARENTING:
The First Four Years

In this and the next chapter we offer age-oriented child rearing suggestions for grandparents tailored from the studies and practical experiences cited in the last chapter. They are distilled from the successes of rational-authoritative parents and sensible grandparents. We emphasize ways in which grandparents can utilize this knowledge to deal with their grandchildren and, at times, assist the parents.

BIRTH TO EIGHT MONTHS

Whatever type of parent you are you can't spoil a little baby. The reason, of course, is that they are born spoiled. All of their needs were met in the uterus and you can't expect them to anticipate anything else. They were held closely all the time. American Indians know this and used papoose baskets to carry their babies most of the time. Aside from the need to be held a lot, the baby also needs to be talked to and to be loved. So what grandmother doesn't really know that? But it's even better to pick up the baby when she isn't crying and fussing. If you only pick her up when she cries, then you condition her to be a cry baby. On the other hand, especially if you or mother or dad happens to be nervous or uptight, sometimes it's better to lay the baby down in a quiet room and let her fuss ten or fifteen minutes. Often the fussing ceases, the baby gives a sigh of relief at escaping the tension she felt in the parent or grandparent and then goes to sleep.

Crying infants create powerful emotions in their parents and grandparents. Pediatric researcher T. Berry Brazelton measured the amount of crying and found that it increases steadily for the first six weeks of life, levels off and then begins to subside. Parents usually learn rather early if the cry is from hunger, thirst, a wet bottom, boredom or pain and then become better able to meet the infant's powerful demands. They do demand of parents! And as grandparents know well, it isn't always easy being a new parent. It's even harder for a new mother and father to become a team, even on how to respond to the baby's cry. Both arrive at their status of parenthood with very different backgrounds, attitudes and experiences. We all tend to be captives of our inner child of the past, directed more by our deep distant experiences, emotions and genetic personalities than by logic. The psychologist research team of Cowan and Cowan laid it out nicely:

"In our work with partners becoming parents it seems clear that men and women begin their journey toward parenthood as if they were on separate trains heading down different tracks, hoping somehow to reach the same destination — the formation of their family. Beginning with markedly different biological points of origin, spouses' different routes through childhood ensure their arrival at adulthood with different gender identities, role behavior, judgments, personality traits, and attitudes."

Your own adult child's inner-child-of-the-past reflects you. At least it reflects how she was raised by you, or believes she was raised by you. Sometimes grandparents have trouble seeing this. Facing ourselves, or our child's image of us, can be disturbing. But how she acts isn't always due to the way you raised her. Certainly we did have an effect. But her personality may spring from her unique genetic traits. Personality evidences itself at birth and must be part genetic, often similar to mother's or dad's or great aunt Susie. Grandparents usually note this and occasionally such history allows a better understanding of a child's behavior and the parent's response.

It always helps to praise positive parenting efforts. And it may be more helpful to bite your tongue if you see nothing positive. Honey does catch more flies than vinegar. New parents need praise and support more than criticism. Anyway, they will learn more from what you do than from what you say. They may not be perfect, but then you probably weren't perfect either. Still, things some parents do need changing.

If your daughter or son-in-law puts their one month old baby in the crib and he cries for an hour and they show no sign of picking him up, how do you handle it? Rather than scold, frown or criticize why not smile and ask politely if they mind if you go in and hold the baby for a while. Say, "It has been a long time since I had the opportunity to hold and cuddle a little one and I appreciate your giving me the chance. I'll try not to spoil him." Not every mother or grandmother is a cuddler, some are and some are not. Possibly grandmother could be a cuddler and mother a non-cuddler. If you are a cuddler you can offer a positive model, a sort of postgraduate teaching session by example, without trying to overpower them with unasked for advice, disapproval or lecturing. After all, while he may be your grandchild, he is the parents' child. New parents' insecurity makes them especially sensitive to any suggestion that they aren't doing things perfectly.

In the example above we discussed crying by a one-month-old infant where allowing an hour of crying would be excessive. By twelve months many babies have to cry it out for even more than an hour if they are to ever develop good sleep or nap habits. Familiarize yourself with the current guidelines and prepare for differences in advice between the experts, and possibly between you and your adult-child and spouse. They do have the final say and grandparents learn to be very diplomatic in offering advice.

Parental insecurity increases with parental fatigue. As you well remember, being up at night for the first two months after coming home from an exhausting labor and delivery can be difficult. Also mother's low hormone level may lead to postpartum blues. At this stage they really need support but they also are more sensitive than usual. Well meant advice can be received as criticism. A good approach is, "What can I do to help?" and then just quietly get busy and help. Having mother available for advice, whether given or not, is comforting.

Young mothers often become exhausted trying to keep the house clean, feed the baby and be on "best behavior" because family and friends pour in to see the new arrival. Few parents haven't been so stressed in the middle of the night that when the baby cries they almost feel like throwing the little devil out the window or walking away and leaving him. Pediatricians explaining this to expectant mothers smile and say, "Just don't throw him out the window and you have it made!" Then they point out the guilt feelings which occur when you get angry at a baby you love so deeply and intensely. Worn out parents need quiet support and comfort, help with the housework and occasionally baby sitting relief. They need this more than direct child care by grandparents. If you can't be there perhaps you can pay for help during the first few weeks while mother recovers.

Betty

The pediatrician, while doing the physical on Betty's infant boy at the two week check up, noted how stressed she looked. The baby was fine but mother was more than tired. "How are you coping with being up all night feeding the baby?" he asked. "I'm exhausted," Betty replied, tearing up and turning her head away in embarrassment.

"Do you have any help? Are your folks or your husband's folks around? Or will one of them come?"

Betty's tears cascaded down her cheeks, "Mother and Dad live in Dallas. They have a business and she helps him. She says she can't leave him alone. I guess the business is more important than me!" she concluded bitterly.

Some parents need even more than help around the house. If they seem too agitated or emotional, keep in mind that they may need to be babied a little themselves. None of us ever outgrow the need to be babied, to be loved and taken care of. And some new parents may even feel a bit jealous that everyone's attention is focused on the baby. They won't admit it of course. Yet it sometimes creates tension. The roots of many divorces start when a new baby is born. Even parents who don't feel jealous or tense still need some babying, some personal and positive attention, understanding and support. So do the new baby's brothers or sisters. They suddenly get less attention. Grandparents really shine here with offers like, "Can I take Jimmy to the zoo today?"

Try to do something for each individual in the family that he or she likes, either for mom or dad separately or together. Look on it as a sort of reward for their giving you a grandchild and contributing to the family tree and to the future of the nation. Don't think so much of what you would like to do for them, think of what *they* need, want or can use. Practical help is more appreciated than a lot of advice. It's reasonable to ask them what they want before you start on a project or decide to go shopping for them. It doesn't hurt to give a hug and a smile, even some sympathy so they recognize that you understand their feelings and appreciate their stress. Be available and receptive for questions. But don't always volunteer advice or even answers, or try to show off your knowledge. It may even help build the confidence of your grandchild's parents by admitting that you don't know everything, even if they ask.

Some parents love their baby so madly they are jealous and even resent sharing the baby with grandparents. While most young couples welcome grandparents' advice and appreciate the interest, not everyone reacts the same. Yet even the "madly" jealous parent usually welcomes being able to get away from baby on occasions when grandmother babysits. Our grandparenting maturity usually enables us to put up with the "mad" or unreasonable emotional reactions of our children or sons-or-daughters-in-law. Let it be their problem. A cool and objective reaction usually allows the situation to settle down and enables us to continue to build on the relationship with the grandchild. Your low key input may, in the long run, be even more important when parents seem irrational. You become a model of restraint and wisdom. Keep a low profile and a tough hide.

All the problems don't come from the parents. Some grandparents just don't relate well to newborns or infants. Let's face it, some people do not like babies at all — even a few pediatricians! Frequently this results from the lack of love we received when we were infants or children. Our own parents, our grandchildren's great grandparents, may not have known how to give love. We carry our inner-child-of-the-past with us to heaven. The emotional conditioning which helped shape our personalities can be hard to overcome. And it's hard to baby a baby if we didn't experience being babied ourselves when we were young. But it is time to break the cycle and improve our parenting and grandparenting methods.

Some grandfathers have problems in relating to babies. This comes from the traditional conditioning of boys in the U.S.. Boys were expected to be macho and leave infants and children to the women. By contrast, fathers in Japan and Spain are much gentler and often more involved with their children. Many of us grandfathers missed out on the satisfactions inherent in close relations with our own infants and children. But not all grandparents, even grandmothers, want such relations. A grandmother wrote us:

"Here's a word for indifferent grandmothers. 'Loving' and 'grandmother' are bound together in a generalization. This grandmother has no such feelings for what I consider two hyperactive grandchildren (probably normal activity). Of course, I don't agree with my daughter's raising methods — too lenient and as inconsistent as I was. Beyond that, however, I still feel no familial twinges. Would early bonding have made a difference? They live a thousand miles away and I see them at most twice a year. They are just a couple of kids and I've never been fond of any children, except my own. My mother remarked that she'd wait until they could carry on an intelligent conversation before she passed judgment on how pleased she was. I think her version of 'intelligent' conversation came a lot earlier than mine will. I will be interested to see my reaction to any future grandchildren I may have, or in the future when those I have mature."

Here is a grandmother who had a critical parent herself and her conditioning or personality makes it hard to relate to little ones. Her inner-child-of-the-past still effects her relationship with her grandchildren and children, and this was probably passed on by her own grandmother. But it's never too late to try. For example, Pediatrician T. Berry Brazelton who enjoys and does research on infants has a message for fathers about helping with the newborn, "Try it, you'll like it!" Not only may you really enjoy it, it can be a growth promoting experience for you. The intimacy of child rearing influences greatly the growth and development of adults. Adults who have not raised children are deprived of an important force for their own maturation. Nothing forces us to grow up like being a parent. It is never too late. The same can be said for grandparents. Later we will offer some suggestions for grandparents who have overactive and distant grandchildren. It's never too late to try, to hold your grandchild and open your heart to him. It is never too late to open our mind to valuable new information about raising children.

THE NINE TO THIRTY SIX MONTH OLD CHILD

Most of us recognize the need to civilize children. However, permissive parents don't insist on good behavior and don't control their children adequately. Most of these children grow up poorly socialized. Perhaps uncivilized is a better word. They don't learn to accept the necessary demands and controls of society very well. They often remain in a dependent state expecting people or society to take care of all their needs and wants, just as their parents did. On the other hand, the excessive demands and harsh discipline of authoritarian parents leads to "squashing" the boys, many of whom become incompetent. They often lack initiative and motivation and become dependent on outside "authority" figures or, conversely, rebel and become almost mindless emotional city hall fighters. Good lessons. But how do you apply these findings to the second and third years of life? Research in the Harvard Preschool Project, later applied by the Missouri Public Schools in the Parents As Teachers Program offers help.

Burton White, in the Harvard Preschool Project, searched for answers to the question of whether preschoolers can be parented in a way to increase their competence and intelligence. His team studied an average mix of parents and children. Their objective measures of parenting during the crawler/toddler stage turned up significant information. It was found that by observing parenting methods, they could predict which fifteen-month-olds would turn out to be best developed and with the highest I.Q. at age three. Measures of three-year-olds can predict which six-year-olds and beyond will do better in school. Overall the children of rational-authoritative parents developed a greater than expected I.Q., above average language development and more competence regardless of the parents educational or socioeconomic level. So, how do you parent and grandparent to achieve such results? Rationally and authoritatively. This requires, first, that you are there to parent or to grandparent — you are there to respond to the child.

Firstborn children receive twice as much parenting time and attention as later-born children and firstborns turn out statistically to be more competent. Enthusiasm on the part of the mother about the child's development seems to be a major factor. Looking at tired mothers with two or more children, or a single working mother, there can be no question but that enthusiastic time from a grandparent may have a profound salutary effect. It may be that the second child needs it from the grandparent more than the first. The effect of enthusiastic attention appears to be maximal for the child in the nine to twenty-four-month age range. White's team found several types of parental attention which have a marked stimulating effect.

One productive way of giving attention to the toddler is to be his consultant, not his boss. Little ones must develop their power. A delicate balance exists in how parents balance this need with the necessary control over the child. Rational-authoritative parents are firm, demand obedience and follow through with action to enforce their demands. At the same time, they allow the child the freedom to explore on his own and enthusiastically respect the child's progress and wishes. These parents serve more as a consultant to the child than a director or dictator. They first create a baby-proof house so the child can explore freely without a whole world of "No's." They facilitate this exploration with stimulating objects such as cardboard boxes, empty spools, plastic pans, balls and spoons. Grandmother's home is rich in all of these educational accoutrements. When it is baby-proofed and expensive lamps which may be broken are moved out of harms way, and after it is poison and accident proofed, it makes a great place for children.

Most importantly rational-authoritative parents and sensible grandparents respect the child enough so that they talk about what the child is interested in at the moment. When the child turns to mother or grandmother for help, he usually gets help, or at least recognition and an explanation that you are busy but will be there soon. Respond enthusiastically to every accomplishment, be it as simple as putting a ball into a box or as complicated and exciting as the first step or first word.

The *way* you talk to a child can significantly increase his language ability. These methods are outlined in Table 4-1. The key seems to be grandmother's or mother's ready availability. Most of the interchanges with the child were brief, perhaps thirty seconds. The total time in a day actually spent directly with the child averaged around two and one-half hours. When mother cannot be there or when her time is taken up chasing after the first child, a real opportunity exists for you as a grandparent to have a positive effect on your second grandchild's ultimate competence.

Table 4-1

**CHARACTERISTICS FOR
ENHANCED LANGUAGE LEARNING***

1. The child between 9 and 24 months of age usually initiated about ten interchanges an hour with her parents during typical daytime activities. The parents usually initiated a similar or smaller number of exchanges. (With first-born children, parents initiated more exchanges than were evident when later-born children were involved.)

2. The parents took the time to identify the interest of the child.

3. Words and appropriate actions, focused on the child's interest, usually followed.

4. The words used were at or slightly above the child's apparent level of comprehension.

5. Full sentences, rather than single words or brief phrases, were the norm.

6. Related ideas were introduced often.

7. Most interchanges lasted between twenty and thirty seconds. Lengthy teaching sessions were rare.

8. Stories were read often, but the child's attention did not become sustained until well into the second year. For a few months after the child's first birthday, picture books were habitually used for "labeling" sessions.

---

* White, Burton PhD, Educating the Infant and Toddler, Lexington, MA: DC Heath and Company, 1988.

Should You Try To Teach Your Grandchild To Read At This Age?

No, but. . . an opportunity exists to help him. Books proposing that parents should teach their two-year-old to read probably create more harm than good. Grandfather Bolton tried to teach Ronald how to read when Ronald was a year and a half old. He used the flash card technique. The teacher is supposed to ask, "What does this word say?"

For the two-year-old, desperately striving for a lever to use to exert his will on the world of giants surrounding him, the easiest answer is to turn the head away. "You can't make me say that!" is the unsaid message given with a look. If he is able to memorize the word and produces a rote reply to the parent's demand, the parent wins. If he ignores the parental demand, which he has the power to do, then he wins. By refusing to be pressured to "repeat after me" demands or requests by his giants, he retains his self respect.

Children learn what and when they want to learn, especially the preschooler. Formal attempts to impose learning on preschoolers may squash the children's initiative. Developing initiative and self motivation is at least as important as the subject to be taught. So, for preschoolers we generally should try to follow their lead and wait for their interest in a subject to manifest itself. If we don't wait we often create resistance. If we do wait we can usually help them learn to read early in childhood.

The time is ripe when Sue brings her favorite book to you. Set her in your lap and always move your finger under the words and sentences from left to right when reading. This starts Sue tracking sentences from left to right. Otherwise many children try to read backwards, from right to left. A good percentage reverse words when they try to write and often will write a mirror image of a word. Helping Sue develop the habit of moving through words and sentences left to right becomes the first way you can help her learn to read. At the same time you help her develop initiative and increase self motivation and self esteem by responding to her and doing what she wants to do. You can also increase Sue's reading ability by offering her the opportunity to read.

As you move your finger along the sentence reading a favorite story aloud to her, possibly for the third time, give her the opportunity to say the word. For example you read, "The cow jumped over the _____." Hesitate as you point to the word moon. If Sue proudly fills in, prompting you by saying "moon", respond enthusiastically with a, "Great! Sue knows how to read!" and continue on with the story.

Hesitate occasionally at different words, giving her the opportunity to say the word herself while your finger points to the word. A few two-year-olds and a good number of three- and four-year-olds will learn to recognize words and know their meaning using this technique. It can be a golden moment when they first start.

You will be tempted to then rush to Mother and Father and proudly say, "Sue can read! Look, Sue, tell Daddy what that word says!" Frequently such a demand to perform is met with that, "Ha! You can't make me say it!" distant stare. The child feels more powerful by demonstrating that she is not a puppet. She doesn't want to respond to the pulling of strings, to become a Charlie McCarthy manikin mouthing the words you point to. Instead, proudly tell the parents, "Sue read the word moon in her book. I think she can learn to read really soon. Won't that be fun for her!" Explain the technique and how you waited until Sue brought the book to you. Laugh with the parents about the two-year-old philosophy, the great importance two- and three-year-olds attach to "I'll do it myself!"

Civilizing The Toddler

Chasing a toddler around can be exhausting and we have seen grandparents breath a sigh of relief after finishing a few hours of "baby sitting." Sitting doesn't seem the appropriate word. Often you need track shoes and vitamins! But a reasonably disciplined toddler in a baby-proof house doesn't create as much stress and fatigue as an undisciplined one or one in a house with too many breakable or dangerous things to get into. If it's your house, baby-proof it. And it's a good idea to have some syrup of ipecac on hand to use in case of accidental poison ingestion, as well as the pediatrician's and poison control's telephone numbers. If the toddler swallows a poison and you give the ipecac promptly, they usually vomit the poison before they absorb it. But call before you use it. If mother uses rational-authoritative methods and the little one will obey, it makes things easier. If not, you might give her a book such as *Love and Power — Parent and Child* which can help her realize the necessary and relatively easy methods of control.

Little ones vary, and some will always test the limits. So even if he will obey mother, he may decide to see if he can get away with disobeying you. Who knows, maybe you're a patsy and he can show his power by ignoring or flaunting your commands. *One of the first things you need to do is establish the ground rules with mother and father.* Agreement helps. Usually consistent discipline gives the best results. But somehow you must be able to exert control — both to keep the explorer alive and to prepare him to get along well with the rest of the world.

The first principle of control is to mean what you say and not use words or tone to punish or vent your frustration. Smart little ones soon figure out that they can ignore verbal abuse. So if you say it, follow through and *act*. Don't keep repeating an admonition over and over and not follow through. Avoid using too many "No's." Look at it from the view of a baby. Little ones by fifteen months often develop a song, "No, no, no, no . . ." Mother, who used to be nice, goes around all day chanting 'No.' They figure that "She hates me, I know because the 'No' is scolding and angry." Naturally, if they have spirit, they will hate her back.

Scolding can lead to deliberately doing those things which make the toddler's giant angry, demonstrating that the little one got his licks in, used his power to push mother's (or grandmother's) button with considerable satisfaction. Around fifteen months, children become very aware of the power imbalance which exists. They live in a world of giants who pick them up, take them away from interesting things like the ashes in the fireplace, poke food in their mouth and generally overpower them. But they want to be big and important and free. Naturally they mimic you and it is humorous to see a fifteen-month-old child scolding mother and telling her "No!" After all, if it worked on the child why not use it on mother to make her mind. And it helps develop a child's self confidence to occasionally make the giants in his world mind. It increases the child's experience in the use of power. But it is a balance — a two-way street. Let them lead you and make you mind at times while overall, you still control the child.

Raising children involves using your powers of both reward and punishment. The power of rewards offers the nicest way to control. Applaud and appreciate good behavior and occasionally even give a tangible reward. But keep in mind that even the good child will do bad things — say like chewing on a light cord with the resulting problem of electrocution or burns. Such behavior requires action. This action is best announced with a firm (but not scolding or angry) "No" followed by prompt removal from the light cord. If it tasted good to him or if he appreciated the attention he got for that behavior, he may head right back to the light cord. In that case, repeat the "No" and add, "No, or grandmother will. . ." The punishment, *which should be agreed upon in advance by his parents*, should be one of two types — isolation or spanking. He is too young to make taking away privileges work. Scolding and hollering makes him think you are angry at him and hate him. You discipline because you love him and must control him, so don't scold. Scolding gives a message that you hate him. It can become verbal abuse and create conflict rather than control.

One effective punishment is putting a toddler in jail. The playpen, without toys, makes a very effective jail. So does the crib. You have to be willing to put up with ten to fifteen minutes of protest by ignoring the crying. White's team found that babies left in playpens too much of the time did not develop quite as well as those allowed to explore the home more freely. But consistent, albeit temporary, "jailing" for refusing to mind can be effective. Later this can be modified into the "time out" technique of putting the child in a chair in the corner.

Grandparents need the permission of the parents to spank, but for most children spanking is an effective punishment if you don't do it in anger. You spank him because you love him, to teach him to obey your "No." So say, "No, or grandmother will spank. No — grandmother spank" to keep his attention while you get a wooden spoon or paint mixing stick. Calmly pull up his pant leg and spank on the calf. When he cries, stop, put the wooden spoon away, and pick him up and give him a love. You don't say you are sorry, instead tell him it's too bad he had to be spanked but that it is his problem, not yours. You spank because you love him and have to teach him to obey.

If you are consistent and follow through, you will hardly ever have to spank or jail. If he knows you mean business, he will generally seek something else to get into. If the home is baby-proofed, you will not have too many things to discipline him about. Get his attention onto more constructive things than being electrocuted or running out into the street in front of a car. And rational spanking is less punishment than the verbal abuse of scolding and hollering.

Most children respond well to:

- Discipline with love and respect.
- Rational punishment.
- Freedom to explore.
- Grandmother or mother as a consultant.

Let The Child Manipulate You

Children (or us adults) don't, in the long run, respond well to scolding and anger. Get them under control in a sensible way, and then you can use your time with less stress and fatigue to encourage the child's development. The first step, a new word, getting a cupboard door open by himself all deserve enthusiastic praise. Reading to him for a minute or two when he brings a book to you is often more valuable than trying to read to him a half hour when *you* want to read to him. Encourage him by letting him lead. Reward his initiative. If he takes you to the next room, if he gets help when he asks you, it helps him develop initiative, self-motivation, self-confidence, his sense of importance — and his mental abilities. Our reward comes from seeing him blossom and develop and knowing that we helped.

THE THREE YEAR OLD

Whatever their personality or state of discipline, three-year-olds command and deserve grandparent's attention. Children's personalities and abilities blossom at this age. So do their omnipotence complexes. They go through a state – hopefully go through it that is – where they want to be God and want to run the world. Just as it's amusing to watch a 21-month-old try to boss you around so can it be engrossing to watch the often sophisticated ways three-year-olds can use to manipulate grandparents. At times it's amazing to observe the demands of some children. They want it "my way!" and nothing else will do. But most do outgrow the terrible twos enough that they are open to reason.

Reasoning From The Child's Standpoint

Effectively reasoning with a three-year-old requires that you think in their terms, put yourself in their shoes, and look at the world from their standpoint. They are midgets in a world of giants and everyone in their world can do anything they can do better. They reside at the bottom of the totem pole, at the end of the pecking order. They want to be big, powerful and important. But they aren't. So how can they achieve that exalted status? Some use charm. Some fight. Some figure. What they often discover is their power to push your button, get your goat, get you upset. If they can get anyone, especially grandparents, parents or siblings to react emotionally, they have a powerful lever enabling them to have an effect on their world. It becomes a way to exert some control over people. So their ability to get you upset becomes a way of establishing their importance. From their standpoint the "bad" results, be it spanking, scolding or angry withdrawal of gifts demonstrates their power. The pay off in ego satisfaction makes it worthwhile to take the punishment their behavior elicits. The result, you may teach them to do just the opposite of what you want them to do because your being upset when you punish is their reward. So another key to dealing with three-year-olds is to protect your button.

Keeping cool and calm when a child misbehaves is an art, a form of self discipline, and an exercise in self growth. Rationally you know that they are kids, and that kids will be kids. Angelic behavior on their part may even warrant suspicion. So chuckle to yourself at their shenanigans and calmly let them know that they can't get your goat. Instead, teach them that their misbehavior hurts them, not you. Set up neutral discipline so if they do the right thing they win, not just you, and if they do the wrong thing they lose, not you. This way their behavior becomes their responsibility, not someone else's.

The Good Child

Many three-year-olds are dolls, try hard to please and generally get their way by being good. Good for you. That's ok too. Just don't let them con you into doing too much for them or always monopolizing your attention. "Good" children can be just as selfish and manipulative as "bad" children. So return their love, enjoy them, but don't stop demanding that they must be good for themselves by doing the right thing, not just the temporarily pleasing thing to capture your attention as Elisa tried to do.

Elisa

Three-year-old Elisa ran to grandmother as she came in the door, "Grandma, Grandma, you're here! You're here!" She enthusiastically put up her arms for a hug, and at the same time pushed her two year old brother away with her hip. Jack's "Gamaw, gamaw" was lost as Elisa chattered happily away. Grandmother put her down and Elisa grabbed her hand pulling her toward her bedroom to show her how her doll house was arranged. Elisa's mother came from the kitchen wiping her hands on a dishtowel, smiled and gave grandmother a hug, "Gosh Mom, I am glad you could come. Dinner is about ready and Harry will be home any minute now." She turned to Elisa and said, "Stop bothering Grandmother. Give her a minute to catch her breath." Elisa smiled and quieted down. But when Grandmother was handing her coat to mother and little Jack edged over to grandmother's leg, Elisa pushed him away scolding, "Didn't you hear mother? You are bothering Grandma!"

Grandmother reached down and picked up Jack saying, "You get a turn too, don't you Jack." She smiled at Elisa and said, "Neither of you are a real bother. After I give Jack his hug and talk with Mother I will come in and look at your doll house."

By not giving in to Elisa's insistent demands and by sharing her hugs and attention with little brother, Grandmother taught Elisa that she wasn't the only one deserving of attention and love. A simple action and a simple lesson, but an important one. If Grandmother had let Elisa selfishly take her entire attention she would not have done her a favor. Selfishness, like most other forms of human behavior, needs control. Rarely should one child be able to monopolize your attention to the exclusion of all others.

Once you have your grandchild's attention and have demonstrated your own power of decision, you can have fun and stimulate his development at the same time. As you know, play for a three-year-old is a consuming activity; serious business. It is the essence of learning day to day living. So play with them, have fun, feed their egos. Try to do as many of the things they want as you can. Let them lead you. Be a ready and willing consultant. But remember that two-year-old Jack probably needs your attention more than Elisa who tends to dominate him and push him into the background. Second children do not get as much of mother's attention as the first child. So, after giving Elisa some attention tell her that Jack needs some of your time and suggest that she arrange her doll house and that you will come back and look at it afterwards. Then let Jack take you to his room, or to the yard or wherever he wants. Let him lead you. Enthuse about his accomplishments. He needs this positive input. It helps him develop his self confidence and competence. If you have to, arrange to have some one-on-one time with him when Elisa is busy doing something else.

The Child Who Misbehaves

The challenges of grandparenting continue. How do you react to bad behavior from a grandchild?

Johnny

Johnny was upset when Grandfather came to visit. He had disobeyed Mother and was sent to his room when he refused to stay in the chair in the corner for his time out. Just released from "jail" the scowl on his face reflected his mood. Normally he liked to play with grandfather and exchange hugs. But today he snapped at him "I don't want to see you!" Grandfather looked calmly at Johnny, shrugged his shoulders and walked by him without a glance, saying as he passed, "Ok." He sat at the kitchen table talking with mother. After a few minutes Johnny came into the room and sat next to grandpaw. Grandpaw continued talking with mother but reached over and gently squeezed Johnny's shoulder. But Johnny, still angry, couldn't contain himself and started banging his hand on the table.

Mother said, "Johnny, stop that or go to your room again," and continued to talk with grandfather. Johnny stopped the banging and after a minute said to grandfather, "Do you want to see my new transformer?" Grandfather briefly said, "I thought you didn't want to see me, Johnny," and continued the conversation with mother. Johnny started to interrupt again but mother stopped him and said, "Johnny, I think that you should say you are sorry for the way you talked to grandfather. Then maybe he will want to look at your transformer after we finish talking."

Johnny hesitated, then hung his head and said, "I really did want to see you grandpaw." Gramps gave him a little friendly squeeze on the shoulder, smiled and said, "I know Johnny. Now run along and when mother and I finish talking you can show me your transformer." Johnny replied, "But grandpaw, I want you to come now!" Grandfather said, in a non-scolding tone, "You will just have to wait. If you interrupt again then I won't be able to look at your transformer at all. Now run along like you were told." Johnny acquiesced, climbed down from the chair and went to the family room to play by himself.

Grandfather's and mother's justified firmness paid off. Had Grandfather given in to Johnny it would have undercut mother's discipline and Johnny wouldn't have learned that he must respect his parents and his elders or pay the price. He also begins to learn that he must, on occasions, delay gratification, a key to productive self control. Stanford researchers found that four-year-olds who were able to delay gratification, in order to get a greater reward later, turned out to be more competent ten years later. It is not certain whether the ability to delay gratification was taught to them or that some children were already smart enough to figure out that this was the best tactic. However, self control and the ability to delay impulsive behavior certainly can be taught as valuable social and academic skills. Three is probably the right age to start. Teaching patience, a natural grandparenting gift, contributes to the child's future competence. Competence and confidence can also be built by encouraging the child's leadership and initiative.

Teaching

If Johnny greets grandfather at the door with a smile and hug, grandfather might give mother a smile and go with Johnny before spending time with mother. Let him lead the conversation and discuss the transformer with him. Give him a bit of history at the same time, "We didn't have transformers when I was a child. But I had a neat red wagon. Once I put a dress on my little dog and put him in the wagon. But she didn't like being in the dress and kept jumping out of the wagon. So I stopped and took off the dress and let her just run along side." You impart important lessons in values as you talk to him yet you don't lecture down at him from a position of power. Johnny at age three is on his own power trip and he may try to demonstrate his power by thwarting you by not listening to you, utilizing the technique of "grandparent deafness."

While we can get further communicating with Johnny at his level we need to keep in mind the old saying, "Children should be seen but not heard." This plum of ancient wisdom contains considerable truth. If Johnny retains center stage, is first in line and the center of attention all the time then no need exists for him to grow up and act adult. Those children who do not get their omnipotence complexes under control become very hard to live with. So it behooves grandparents not to spoil Johnny by always letting him have his way or always being center stage.

Grandfather, after playing and talking with Johnny for awhile said, "Johnny, I am going to talk with your mother now. You stay here and play. Mother and I have adult things to discuss." Johnny made a face and clung to grandfather's coat. "But I want you here" he whined. Grandfather firmly disengaged his hand from his coat and walked out of the room. Johnny followed, whining. Grandfather sat at the table with his daughter. Mother said, "It sounds like Johnny is tired and needs a nap. What do you think?" Grandfather nodded and said "I think you're right. He sounds tired." Mother said, "Johnny, go to your room and lay down. Come out when you feel less tired and don't have to whine." Johnny protested that he wasn't tired and just wanted grandpa to play with him. Mother said, "Johnny, if you don't go now I will have to put you in your room and lock the door. Now, will you go as I told you or do I have to take you. Mother and grandpa are going to talk now. Run along."

Working With Mother

Grandfather should go along with whatever action mother takes and avoid openly criticizing mother. In this day and age especially, most mothers tend to be a bit insecure about how they raise their children. Often they resent interference even more because of their uncertainty. It's easy for grandfather to feel sympathy and go play with Johnny. But this teaches him that whining pays off. And it not only would undercut mother's authority, it also gives Johnny too much power to manipulate by negative behavior. If mother won't act, then ignore Johnny and just talk with her. Your action speaks louder than words. Johnny is not allowed to interrupt adult conversations successfully. He must learn to respect his parents and grandparents.

Permissive Parents

If the parents are too permissive then grandfather may subtly establish some control and limits by saying, "Johnny, your whining won't help. You had better go play while mother and I talk. If you don't act big enough to mind then I won't be able to give you the toy I bought for you yesterday. It's for boys who can act bigger than you are acting today." If Johnny doesn't heed your advice then don't give him a toy that day. Wait until he behaves more "grown up." You can't always take over for a permissive parent, but at least you can exert your own influence and educate him a bit about how the world outside the family will most likely treat him. Exert your influence and use your power to avoid rewarding misbehavior. Johnny will respect you for such action even if he argues or sulks. Keep your word – be reliable and powerful. This gives him a model for self control and teaches him that he cannot manipulate or run over the world like he runs over his mother. His underlying search for limits is rewarded by your neutral firmness.

Your effectiveness in such teaching depends to a large degree upon your attitude. Don't let his misbehavior be your problem. It will be if you react with hurt, anger or disgust. Deliver your message, both in words and body language, in a neutral manner. Follow through with action, such as simply taking the toy back home with you. No reason exists for you to get upset. It's his loss, not yours.

Authoritarian Parents

If the parent's discipline is too authoritarian and Johnny never gets a chance to stand up for himself, then it lowers his chance of becoming a competent adult. If his parents are harsh and act angry with him a lot, you may subtly counter balance their harshness by listening to him attentively and trying to play with him and talk with him. Sometime this has to be when mother and father are not around. Take him for a walk or a ride down to the park. Some authoritarian parents call this spoiling; actually it helps Johnny develop his self-confidence by being able to manipulate adults, even to occasionally argue with them and win if he is right. This ability to stand up for himself against "authority" figures who demand immoral or unwise behavior will stand him in good stead when he is out of the reach of the family.

So even under difficult conditions grandparents keep on parenting by example, by their actions and attitudes. Parenting really is forever. Every contact with a grandchild leaves an impression and has an effect. You can help your grandchild's development best by using rational-authoritative grandparenting methods. He can become more competent. You will be better able to pass on treasured and important values. If nothing else, you discipline the permissively raised grandchild by not permitting him to run over you. The punishment emphasizes withdrawal of privileges and refusal to be manipulated or bullied by misbehavior.

Being A "Grand" Parent

In most cases isolation, by either removing the child or yourself, represents a useful tool. In all cases warmth toward the child in tone and action should continue. Love is unconditional. Approval and rewards on the other hand are very conditional. But set up your discipline so the child's actions are his responsibility and affect him far more than they affect you. Help him learn that he must take the consequences of his actions, good or bad. This teaches him the lesson that he is responsible for himself. Even bratty children will thank you for this lesson in the future. In some cases you may be the only positive reality in a grandchild's life and you offer him a path to follow. One person, even outside a family, can have a major impact on a child's life. Your opportunity as a strong and loving "grand" or "super" parent allows you to offer leadership and meaning to his life.

5 SENSIBLE GRANDPARENTING
From Four Years to Young Adults

FOUR-YEAR-OLDS

Four-year-olds are remarkable little creatures. Their curiosity begins to broaden. They become more aware of the world, of the people in it, and of their vulnerability. They have minds like sponges and a capacity that should not be wasted. They learn what they want to and when they want to learn it. But much of the world they learn about comes from television, from violent cartoons, and from groups of children in the neighborhood or day care. Their energy tends to wear us out. But they can be lovable and enjoyable. Yet at times they seem hostile and challenge their parents, and even their grandparents.

Hostility

By the age of four most children find that the darned world doesn't mind them very well. Their omnipotence complex, their desire to be boss, rubs up against all of those other people's desire to be boss too. This lack of respect, which is how the four-year-old usually sees it, creates hostility. So he gets angry at a world that doesn't obey him. How angry and how hostile he becomes depends upon his temperament. But grandparents have mellowed and find it easier to recognize that hostility at this age occurs naturally. Here a golden opportunity exists for grandparents to help the child develop a sense of the value of self control. Not getting hostile in return is the first step — this demonstrates an admirable model of maturity and self control.

Sue

Four-year-old Sue's frown still creased her forehead when she and grandmother walked into the playground. Sue still felt like going back home and hollering at mother. Mother was "very unreasonable," making her apologize to grandmother and before that scolding her for leaving a mess in the hall! Sue thought the mess wasn't that bad and that mother had no business swatting her when she told mother that she wouldn't pick up her things. Mother was angry and that's when grandmother arrived. Sue was angry when her grandmother came in and said "Hello," so Sue turned her back on her. This made mother even angrier and she made Sue apologize and then sent her to her room.

After awhile mother let Sue out of her room but the tension in the house was high. Grandmother asked if Sue wanted her to take her to the nearby park, thinking that getting her away would clear the air. Sue mumbled yes while shooting a look of malice toward mother. Mother, exasperated but relieved, agreed. Sue went but kept quiet during the walk to the park. Grandmother sat quietly on the bench and Sue went to the rings and began swinging along. Another girl was ahead of her and Sue had to drop off. She angrily pushed the other girl and said, "Get out of my way!" At that grandmother got up, walked over and took Sue's hand firmly and said, "Sue, tell that little girl that you are sorry." Sue mumbled a muted "sorry" and grandmother marched her over and sat her on the bench next to her. Grandmother then looked at Sue quizzically and said, "My goodness, you certainly are in a bad mood today. Did you get out on the wrong side of the bed? Or did all this start because you wouldn't do what your mother asked and pick up your mess in the hall?"

Sue wiggled a bit and defensively said, "I was going to pick up my toys later." Grandmother calmly replied, "Sue, did you hear about my neighbor Mrs. Kennedy breaking her leg?. . ." Sue looked up out of the corner of her eye and shook her head. "Well," grandmother said, "her son Johnny left some toys on the kitchen floor and Mrs. Kennedy didn't see them. She tripped on them and fell and broke her leg. It hurt awfully and she had to go to the hospital, have shots for the pain and was in a cast for four months. It was miserable for her. . . I guess that's one reason why parents insist that kids pick up their toys."

Grandmother looked at the swings and said, "Oh, look, a swing is empty now. Do you want me to push you? OK, let's go."

Grandmother's calmness, self control and firmness all taught Sue a lesson and offered her a model of adult behavior. Even though Sue had misbehaved, that was over with. Grandmother could be fun. Her actions and story had made the point so she went on to other things and didn't dwell on the misbehavior. No grudges, no scolding, no anger. She acted sensibly and with authority letting Sue's problems be her own, not Grandmother's.

Fears

Four-year-olds become quite aware of the outside world. It's big. And they learn about some of the dangers like cars and kidnappers. Television brings the seamy side of the world into the family room day after day — violence becomes routine. Around this time children become acutely aware of the vulnerability of their bodies. They enter the bandaid era. A scrape, especially if they can see it, becomes a catastrophe. An earache, well, it hurts but it's out of sight. At the same time they enter the monster stage and are fascinated by heroes who can protect them from monsters. Some of us don't outgrow these feelings completely and still want superman, or his political equivalent, to help us face the rigors of life.

A major fear of childhood underlies and stimulates the four-year-old preoccupation with fear – the possibility of separation from home and mother and father. Children know they couldn't make it on their own in that big world out there. This basic fear usually peaks around the age of four. The need for security it engenders has given rise to many of the great novels of childhood. The classic story of Heidi in the Swiss Alps, orphaned and then essentially abandoned by her aunt, featured a crusty old Grandfather who saved the day. Later, with Grandfather's help Heidi was safely adopted by a new and wonderful set of parents. Grandparents play a role in fact in reducing childhood fears. They are an actual safety net for children both in promise and sometimes in practice.

Another aspect of separation fears involves growing up. If you grow up you leave home! That's dangerous and unacceptable. The child becomes aware of this inevitability and begins looking for a way out. Many come up with the bright idea that they will marry Mom or Dad and thus stay home forever. This fear of growing up and becoming adult may be greater in nuclear families with no grandparents around. If grandparents, uncles, aunts and cousins visibly exist in the extended family network, the separation fears may ease a bit. If the family limits stop at mother, father and child then the child loses the valuable safety net of the extended family. Large cohesive families reduce anxieties about abandonment. Families today are too small and too dispersed for enough family security and stimulation. In the future unsettling events will probably increase. A report issued in 1990 by the Worldwatch Institute on the State of the World warned that unless things change dramatically over the next few decades, ". . .we'll be in a situation where environmental degradation and economic decline will begin to feed on each other". . .as population increases, more farm land is lost and the greenhouse effect becomes a reality. This offers good reason for grandparents to double their efforts to be linked with their children and grandchildren. Large extended families can tough it out together far better than isolated nuclear families.

Because of separation fears, the greatest fear of all becomes the fear of the ultimate separation — death. When children find this can happen they worry about it, probing it like a slightly sore loose tooth — question, question, question. "Can we call grandma long distance in Heaven?" "Why won't my kitty come back?" You may have the child convinced that he will go to heaven in a golden Cadillac with harps being played on the way, but he is not about to leave. Few adults feel ready, but for the child it simply does not compute — it's too threatening. So they bury it and quit talking about it. Often this leads to strange fears or nightmares which represent suppressed death fears.

Tiffany

Tiffany's grandfather had died a few months before her fourth birthday. Mother had explained that Grandfather was with God and couldn't come to their house anymore. Just before Tiffany's birthday she and Mother were making out the guest list. Mother asked her who she wanted to come to her birthday party and Tiffany started crying. "Why are you crying, honey?" asked her puzzled mother. Tiffany wiped her tears on her sleeve, sniffled and replied, "Cause I want Grandpa and God to come to my party!"

Some children announce that they are not going to grow up. Why? "Because if you grow up you get old and you die!" Thus the Peter Pan myth protects, for in it one goes to Never Never Land and doesn't have to grow up. Grandparents do not represent Never Never Land but they can help, first by being actively involved with the grandchildren. That, by example, can make growing old not a terrible thing. Second, if you project an image of a lack of fear of death the sting lessens. The loss a child feels when a grandparent dies can also be lessened by the time you spend with him while you can. Grandparents leave many living memories and a legacy of support and guidance.

Mary

We ran across Mary, a freshman at Stanford, at a retirement home. She spends an hour or so a week visiting elderly people in her area. Her grandmother had been around her most of her life so she learned to enjoy and appreciate the companionship and wisdom of the elderly. Her fellow students, most of whom probably had little contact with grandparents, never think of visiting the elderly. Those unfamiliar with the comfort and value of their elders may, in fact, shun old people. Being old, facing death, becomes taboo.

Grandparents should probably not bring up the subject of death around children under the age of ten to twelve. If the subject does come up it shouldn't be dwelled upon. Be truthful but leave out details and embellishments. Still, it helps to offer the model of mature acceptance of aging while enjoying life, yet not fearing death. However the most important way of meeting the issue involves giving our grandchildren positive and valuable memories and values by which we, in a fashion, live beyond death. Grandparents who face death can present a model of comfortable acceptance of the inevitable. We can't live forever. Facing our maker without fear helps remove some of the sting for both us and our grandchildren. But grandchildren, especially young ones who are close, often become angry about losing a grandparent. It is a loss to the child. That in itself confirms our importance — it validates the efforts we make in grandparenting. The good memories left behind help children realize that calm acceptance of the inevitable means that life is good, grandparents are admirable, and death becomes less fearful.

THE FIVE-YEAR-OLD

Five-year-olds want to be big and important, a state incompatible with being little and afraid. So they get their fears under control and take a major step toward separating from their parents. They go to school. While they are usually proud and eager, underneath it all they often feel anxious and homesick. So they rush home after school wanting more love and attention. They say in effect, "You can pour it on me by the bucket and I still won't have enough." Mother and father, the primary source of security, spend a lot of time with each other. Some children think, "Look at all that time they waste on each other when I want it!" Often they haven't given up the idea of marrying mother or father to assure their position in the family in the future. At this stage they frequently make an effort to get their way by playing mother and father apart. As a grandparent if you notice your grandchild trying to do this you can help the parents cope by telling them a personal story about this common behavior.

Sue

"I couldn't help but smile, Sue, when Jessica smirked at you because she got to sit in her dad's lap the other night. It reminded me of when you were about this age. You told me that you were going to marry dad when you grew up and that I could come and visit. Then you got mad because both dad and I couldn't help but laugh."

Stories such as Sue's allows the parents some understanding of the child's need to manipulate. It can also help mother and father become a team. If you were a reasonably successful parent yourself tell them how you and your wife used to set aside a time with each other once a week to discuss how the children did in the past week and what to expect in the coming week. This allowed you to come to an agreement on how to handle the inevitable problems without being played apart. You can say that you learned it from your pediatrician. This removes the unwelcome feeling that you are trying to interfere and overpower the parents. Later let them think that it is their idea. You can get a lot accomplished if you don't mind who gets the credit.

The Need

Five-year-olds really need grandparents. Some of them need all the help they can get. A few have such a fear of leaving that they decide not to go to school. School phobia requires determined parental action. The child must be forced to go. Often grandparents can help by taking the child to school if mother works — or by being there when school is out so somebody's home. Neighborhoods can organize a "block watch" function for school children coming home. Grandparents, with or without their own grandchildren in the area, may want to organize the neighborhood or volunteer to be available to the kids and keep an eye out for potential problems.

The process of weaning a child away from home can be difficult. Sometimes it helps both mother and child to relate a story about a person you knew who went through the same ordeal and survived. Call attention to an individual who had school phobia as a child and is now, say, an air force jet pilot or some such powerful figure. It points out the reward inherent in going to school, helps the child's self esteem by showing that strong people were fearful too and got over it. It offers a model to emulate.

Values

One of the roles of grandparents is to expose grandchildren to the values of the past and the continuity of enduring customs. Mostly we do this by the way we act, what we are and what we say but direct education is also needed. In the past, and still for the majority of the world's population, this was a recognized grandparental duty. But who does it now? During our time, the last half of the twentieth century, old values and their sources were challenged as never before. Columnist Walter Lippman wrote: "No mariner ever enters upon a more uncharted sea than does the average human being born in the twentieth century. Our ancestors knew their way from birth through eternity; we are puzzled about the day after tomorrow." This uncertainty creates problems for children. As the end of the century moves toward a close, children seem to get more of their values from people outside the family in day care, in school or after school during long hours watching television. When both parents work children have even less exposure to family values.

Some people argue that we don't or shouldn't select the right values and pass them on to our children or grandchildren. They argue for choices for the individual and for the freedom this entails. Certainly choices must be made and freedom is essential. But at what age should the choice be made, and at what price? What background of experience and education do the children have to make such choices? Is their judgment up to the task? Do we learn from history? There are rules for human living in The Bible and The Koran for example. History tells us not to disregard these fundamentals. These rules seem to favor further evolution. As grandparents we represent history — and one way we can teach values is to teach history.

Religion tends to bring out strong feelings and here the issue of indoctrination comes into play. Some object to indoctrination. But psychologist James C. Dobson argues, "There is a critical period when certain kinds of instruction are possible in the life of the child. . . Their concepts of right and wrong are formulated during this time. . . Permanent attitudes can be instilled during the first seven years of life." When parents say they are going to withhold "indoctrination" from their small child, allowing him to "decide for himself," they are almost guaranteeing that he will decide in the negative. . . The child listens closely to discover just how much his parent believes what he or she is preaching; "any indecision or ethical confusion from the parent is likely to be magnified in the child."

As grandparents we each face the question of how well we passed on our values to our own adult children. Abstract values are usually fixed by 10-12 years of age. Failure to give the child values during this age may be one of the reasons why teenagers are so difficult to change and won't listen. And what about the values of the in-law parents of our children? They too have made their own choices. Grandparents don't have the same rights as parents. Yet we do have a responsibility to let our grandchildren know how we feel and what we value. But we have to live those values if we expect them to have an effect. Small children are very practical. Their bottom line in deciding what values to follow is how you and their parents act. So by just being yourself you offer a model of your real values. It is highly unlikely that a grandparent will succeed in indoctrinating a grandchild without the parent's full agreement and participation. However, children sense quickly that there is a difference between the way grandpa and dad act. This discrimination is one of childhoods most fascinating features, and they do make choices based on their perceptions. By just being around you may offer them another choice.

If a grandmother actually parents the child full time then she might have different rights. This depends to a significant degree on the child's parents' attitudes. Some rejecting neglecting parents, often on drugs or in trouble, don't seem to care. Then grandparents have the right and duty to offer the grandchildren a decent sense of values. As a start they often do this by the fact of taking care of the child, by really parenting. Grandparents who step in and take the child from impossible dysfunctional parents become the grandchild's real parents. Some of the problems facing such grandparents are explored in Chapter 8, Troubled Families.

SIX TO TWELVE

Most six to twelve-year-olds comfortably develop good social values and cruise through school without significant problems. This assumes they live most of the time with people who model good values and demand good behavior. A child needs to have parents around with watchful eyes who use their authority to enforce their demands. At the same time both parents and grandparents should respect and listen to the child. But this doesn't happen for millions upon millions of grammar school children who come home to an empty house. Even if the parents use excellent rational-authoritative child rearing methods, they can't use them if they aren't there. Television hardly substitutes.

Both parents *and* grandparents should learn to care about other people's kids too. In the past, neighbors, tradesmen, even strangers used to keep an eye out for childish misbehavior or problems and would take action if it seemed needed. Playing at another's house expanded contacts with adults of similar background and reinforced their values.

IN YOUR CARE

If you are lucky enough to live near your grandchild's home, maybe you can have him come to your house after school. When and if you do you will be more effective if you use sensible grandparenting methods. The first rule is to be readily available to really listen to and hear the child. He needs a committed adult to talk to, to confide in, to check out what he did and offer approval and guidance. Second, use your authority to clearly set up comfortable rules and enforce them. Have an agreement, established at a conference with mother and father, on what his duties and privileges are at your home. Learning to be a considerate guest is an important social skill for everyone. It isn't out of line to have him do some small chores to help you. And if he studies after school at your home this leaves him more time to interact positively with his parents when they come home. Naturally he needs play, and you may find yourself bringing him to various activities. The most important part of all this is that you are there and available to him if he wants to talk with you.

If They Live Elsewhere

If you live away from your granddaughter and know she is a latch key kid, a routine telephone call after school offers some help. It is better if she can call you. This helps her develop initiative and self confidence. But if she doesn't, call her. Some "really busy" children don't want to spend a lot of time on the phone with a grandparent. Others will talk your ear off. Either way, accept her lead but express your interest. Be especially willing to listen and really hear her. Let her know that you understand her. But make the calls fun, not a chore. One technique is to exchange kid jokes. Call her to deliver your daily joke or to hear hers, whether it is "Why did the chicken cross the road . . ." or "Simon says . . ." etc. This helps break the ice and opens the door to more comfortable conversation.

Ask your grandson how school is going, does he like his teacher, who does he play with and is he enjoying reading or baseball more. If it is baseball maybe you can send him some baseball cards for his collection or newspaper clippings about his favorite team or player. If it is baseball try to see some of his games and, win or lose, celebrate after the game with ice cream!

If you really live too far away to phone or can't afford it, send post cards to her, say, twice a week. Look for funny cards or cards that match her interests. Some children enjoy making a collection of post cards. Ask her to write to you. Give little guys a bunch of stamped postcards with your address on them as a gift so they will be able to write to you easily. Check with mother and father occasionally in the evenings to ask how they and the children are doing. Working parents don't have a lot of time so let them take the lead. Sometimes they will want to talk — other times the call should be brief. Ask if they are busy and be prepared to listen more than pontificate. Don't offer advice unless you are asked to do so. Try to be a real friend, not just the powerful parent. Be alert to their moods and, as much as possible, aware of their needs.

Visits

From six to twelve years is a good age to offer having your grandchild visit or "sleep over" by himself at your home. Make the visit fun but don't hesitate to ask him to help you weed a patch of the garden or vacuum the family room so you will have time to take him to the zoo or a movie. Visits to the library on the way to the store may lead to a worthwhile interest in books. Most children welcome looking at old picture albums, especially if they have pictures of his parents or of him as a younger child. This gives him an idea of what life was like in the "old days" and helps him appreciate his roots. Your keeping his picture demonstrates that you value him. Stories about relatives and friends usually are well received. Sometimes they have to be short. Often they can be triggered by a TV show episode which the child can relate to or to something he tells you about his life. When you get into a story telling mood watch your audience. Some of us tend to "run off at the mouth" and can bore people, including children, by going on too long. During your trips into the past with stories about relatives you may be able to express significant values.

Lap Time

Many children at this age need lap time above all else. Simply sitting him in your lap and holding him may be the best way of communication. We all need to be loved. Most of us still would like a lap to sit on, another person who cares enough, is compassionate and is strong enough to depend upon. The evolution of love starts by being loved yourself and ends with giving love to others. Most grandparents, over time, evolve into very loving and socially responsible individuals even if we didn't all start out that way. We can start our grandchildren on this path early by showing them they are worth loving — by loving them.

Stimulating

Grandparents expand a child's views of the world. Usually the grandparents have different experiences than the parents and sharing these broadens horizons. Children are usually surprised and intrigued by how well their parents remember their own grandparents and like to hear stories about their lives. Sharing these reminiscences while going over picture albums offers a productive way to expand our grandchildren's horizons.

Bob

While the family was together for Thanksgiving grandfather Bob's memory was stimulated by a picture of his own grandfather in the album he was showing the grandchildren. This led to a story about the relations of carving turkeys to the Taj Mahal. Bob's Grandfather Thomas' skill in carving turkeys at holiday dinners was admired by the family. Probably that was because he had their hungry attention on the upcoming meal. As they waited and he carved, he told his captive audience stories of his travels around the world. At one Thanksgiving dinner, while they waited for their serving of turkey, he had told about a visit he had made to the Taj Mahal. This sparked Bob's lifelong wish to visit India. When he got there the Taj Mahal was even better than it had been in his imagination. He described the beauty and aura of this magnificent structure and the fascinating customs and conditions of the people of India. In the process he stimulated another generation's interest in foreign travel.

Controlling your Grandchild

Controlling your six to twelve-year-old grandchildren often represents a challenge. If their parents are permissive they may not expect or respond to your efforts at control and if their parents are authoritarian they may rebel. You have the right to demand certain behavior in your home and car or when you accept the responsibility for the child's care while the parents are gone. Your demands should be firm, low key and without scolding or talking down to the child. State the demand. Ask that he please obey. If he doesn't, calmly give him his options and your options. Then follow through and act. Let it be his problem, his reward or punishment, not yours. He will respect you for your strength and power when you act firmly and fairly. Rarely does the need exist to get angry. But do follow through with the consequences, good or bad. You can exert control more easily when only the child is with you, it becomes more difficult when the parents are there.

Working With The Parents

Your ability to control your grandchild depends to a large degree on the attitude of his parents. You may or may not agree with the way your grandchildren's parents are raising their children — your grandchildren. But you must recognize that most parents are extraordinarily sensitive about their parent's approval or disapproval of their methods of child rearing. Getting along with one's adult-child and spouse on the issue of child rearing can be a very delicate matter. We discuss this in more detail in chapter six and offer other ways to approach the problem. But here you are, concerned about the way your adult-child and spouse are raising your grandchildren. Can you coach them effectively? Some feel that they are trying to raise their children just like you raised them and are hurt if you imply that they aren't. Others have rebelled against what they remember of your methods of child raising and go to the opposite extreme. Some of these parents, your adult children or their spouses, remain very angry and have to hold themselves back from openly criticizing the methods you used in the past.

Even if you did a superb job, the problems they had as adolescents in developing independence, self control and autonomy, the freedom to be an adult out from under your power, may be exacerbated if you attempt to control them now. If, due to the passage of time and the growth of wisdom, you realize that your methods were not the best, admit it and apologize. This may set the stage for discussions on how to do it right — and how you as a grandparent are learning more about parenting. The old saying that you can't teach an old dog new tricks, is a myth. Prove it wrong. This demonstrates your continuing love and dedication to your children and your sincere interest in doing a better job with your grandchildren.

It may be more acceptable to offer "outside" opinions that you have heard or read about on the outcome of various methods of child rearing. One way is to criticize your *own* past methods and offer the opinion that your adult child will probably do better than you did. It can help to joke about your past difficulties. One of John F. Kennedy's most endearing qualities to those around him was his jokes — always told on himself, not on others. Do it in the spirit of love, of fun, and very carefully and diplomatically. Be careful that you pick the right time to offer your opinion. Let it come up naturally. A good time is when they are talking about their problems with parenting and seem open to suggestions. If you do offer your opinions, avoid lecturing, criticizing or scolding.

ADOLESCENCE

Children must pass through the tumultuous period where they cease being children but aren't yet adults. The teen part of the word teenager originally meant grief, pain, revenge. Keeping that in mind helps us understand them; at least it tells us what our ancestors thought of the age. But beware of generalizations. They are unique individuals, each different from each other, at a time when they are trying to find similar friends to group with. Furthermore their physical changes do not always parallel their mental changes, giving rise to unmet expectations from their world. In this trying period they act babyish one day and the next day like a mature grown up. People debate about which portion of adolescence is the worst. Many firmly believe that junior high and the ages of thirteen and fourteen years should be abolished. Others point to the age of fifteen or sixteen as being the nadir of human development, the ultimate in self-centeredness. Adolescents face more traps this day and age than we did and it seems overwhelming to many of them. Instead of entering a structured society with solid values and dependable traditions they find themselves bombarded with conflicting values in a confusing society tempting them with easy ways out. It makes it harder for them to grow up and find their place in society. It may keep them acting "teen" too long: grief, pain, revenge!

Why Teenagers Are Teenagers

The change from a child to an adult takes several steps. To develop responsibility for themselves they first must be empowered to make decisions, to run their own lives. This first step in changing from a child to an adult involves some emotional separation from the parents. From around eleven to fourteen years they struggle to emancipate themselves from direct parental control. This drive for independence comes up against at least four major counterbalances. First, they aren't ready. They can't have their cake and eat it too, they cannot be independent because they are still dependent upon their parents and thus responsible to them. Second, their anxieties and ambivalence about growing up and taking responsibility for their own actions tends to hold them back. Third, the parents need to control them so they don't go too far too fast and get into serious trouble. Fourth, they need societal structure and values which offer a relatively safe and certain path to follow.

To successfully control their anxieties they need self-confidence. Grandparents help by looking for and recognizing the good things about the children, by offering respect. Treating them like adults allows them reason to begin to try to act like adults. Grandparents also help by offering lessons from the past which help define a path to follow into the future. They offer a supportive extended family structure. They also can help the parents, as well as society, to enable a stable and practical future for the young adult. All this smooths the way for the adolescents to conquer their anxieties, understand and accept the necessary controls, and look forward to future independence with confidence.

The next stage of development centers around relating to their own generation. As they develop the necessary confidence in their own independence, they then turn to the challenge of developing a new relationship to their peers, the people they will live with for the rest of their lives. Wise parents and grandparents facilitate this by making their friends welcome at home, by taking them along for local shopping trips or to entertainment events, and even on vacations. Grandparents do this best if they share the teenager's sense of excitement about the world. Recognizing their wonder, curiosity and need to experiment helps facilitate healthy relationships with their grandchildren and their friends. This becomes even more important if the adolescent's parents are too busy to spend much time with their children. It also becomes more important if the grandchild has no friends. Adolescents who feel lonely are more likely to try drugs, feel like hurting themselves and be depressed. They are not as much fun to be around but they especially need your help. A real effort should be exerted by grandparents to help the child by support, understanding and modeling friendly behavior.

Adolescent development involves looking into the future. The questions of career or earning a living and getting an education become increasingly important. Grandparents help by example, by encouraging the teenager to experiment safely and to learn about adult occupations and lives first hand. Arrange to take them to visit friends or acquaintances in different walks of life. Let them get a taste of what plumbers and newspaper reporters, mechanics and lawyers, and others actually do to make a living. If possible, offer some financial help for future education. Take him to events which he might otherwise not see, be it auto races or symphonies, rodeos or museums. Cap it off by having him "help" you plan and take a trip, whether a drive to visit relatives or a vacation to Europe. Lead him into helping with the planning and encourage him to lead you by making as many choices as possible and taking as much responsibility as possible. Treat him as an adult you can depend on. Respect his right to choose, to have his own tastes and opinions whether you necessarily agree or not. Let his decisions be his responsibility, not yours. Be a friend.

Many times being a friend to the teenager is difficult. It can be hard to be friendly when you disapprove of your grandchild's behavior and tendency to take risks. But risk taking is a normal part of adolescence. If she were a friend you would probably share your experiences and knowledge about the issue, and perhaps advise her. You wouldn't likely try to use much power, aside from advice, to stop a friend from most self-defeating behavior. But whether the friend took your advice or not you would most likely still be a friend and respect her right to make that choice and take the consequences. The same attitude helps with the adolescent. They often act immaturely because they are immature. If a really serious threat to her well being exists then it becomes important to act. Grandparents are rarely in a position to effectively forbid. That action, if it is possible, resides with the parents. But honest disapproval and warnings should be offered. If the lesson isn't learned and the potential outcome of immature behavior is serious, then the grandparent may withdraw, "I am not going to stay around while you act that way. Let me know when you get it out of your system." This clearly makes the issue the responsibility of the teenager and nobody else.

You may get further if you note what risky behavior may do to the adolescent's social life right now rather than what it may do in the future, "You know, smoking makes your breath smell bad, even your clothes. Most people don't like the odor of second hand smoke, including me. So please don't smoke in the house when I am here."

Misbehavior

Much of the misbehavior we see in adolescents represents their attempt to grow up. In a way, risk taking lubricates their development. By staying out an hour later than the expected time to come home they take the risk of parental anger but by doing so they assert their right to make their own decisions. If they see that they can make such a decision and are greeted not with anger but with rational explanations of why the parents worry, then their behavior becomes their own responsibility and their problem more than the parent's. They took the risk and now must accept the grounding, and the uncomfortable feeling that they were wrong. But that was their decision, and one thing they must be taught is to make their own decisions — hopefully wisely.

If they are asked to help set the rules for their day to day life, this gives them more reason to follow the rules because then they are acting like an adult. If they only follow the parent's rules they act like a dependent child. If the rules seem to primarily represent a parent power trip, and they obey them, they don't have the opportunity to build their independence. They must practice learning to use their own powers of decision to understand that they are the ones most responsible for themselves.

Grandparents can often handle adolescents better than their parents. Mothers are almost always naturally overprotective. And, as we know, it usually hurts to see the adolescent getting ready to go out into the world. It represents the end of childhood, the end of mothering; it is bittersweet. We as grandparents have been through it all as children, as adolescents, and as parents. Now, as grandparents, we can take a broader view. We usually become more rational and less emotional and parent in a more sensible and authoritative manner avoiding both permissivess or authoritarianism. It is intriguing that the experiences of life generally lead grandparents to become more like the rational-authoritative parent who has been shown by objective observational research to produce the most competent children. Most grandparents learn to parent more sensibly than they did when they were younger. Of course, one of the sensible things they learn is not to brag about it.

Research

We have seen measurements which show that children of rational-authoritative parents become more competent than children of permissive parents. Further measures also revealed that children of authoritative parents have fewer drug problems, partly because they are more effectively controlled. Adolescents need control by parents and by society. Columbia University's Institute of Social Analysis studied the outcome of adolescents in different types of communities over a twelve year period. They found that communities with an accepted social structure and common values offered the best environment for the development of competent adolescents. A survey of 5,000 adolescents in Southern California revealed that unsupervised latch key adolescents suffered twice as much drug abuse as those with mothers at home.

GRANDPARENTS' ROLES

Grandparents can step in and offer an after school sanctuary and supervision for the children of working parents. The bottom line? Too much freedom, too little control and structure leads to poor development and often serious problems for adolescents. But how can grandparents help when they must defer to permissive parents whose adolescents often get out of control and into trouble? Sometimes they can take the adolescent into their home as Steven's grandparents did.

Steve

Steven's mother angrily vented her frustrations to the pediatrician. Steven, sixteen, dressed in black with arms spangled by silver bracelets, ears pierced with multiple ear rings, a silver skull belt buckle just under his paunch, glowered hatefully at his mother from under his pitch-black dyed hair. His pale face grimaced as mother listed a litany of his sins — failure in school, smoking marijuana, refusing to obey, not eating right. Mother believed that she was authoritarian. She hollered at Steve and berated him for his failings. In fact she was permissive. She didn't act, didn't follow through with her recurrent threats. What came through mostly was her anger.

The pediatrician listened as the two argued angrily with each other. The pediatrician finally asked Steve what he wanted to do. Steve sullenly said he didn't want to live at home. When asked where he could go he said he could live with his grandmother. Mother snorted and said, "I don't know if your grandparents will take you the way you act!" The pediatrician offered the opinion that both Steven and his mother might be better off if Steve left home, and urged him to call his grandparents and see if he could live with them.

Steve's grandparents accepted him but carefully laid down the conditions of behavior they would expect from him. These included no drugs, going to school routinely and limited help in their yard. After a few days Steve began acting up. He refused to go to school because he said he was too tired from yard work. So his grandparents told him to leave. He went home for one night, came back to the grandparents the next day and apologized and asked if he could stay with them again. They said yes, but with the same rules. Over the next few months his acting up spells subsided. On the next visit to the pediatrician he looked less stressed and less angry.

Steve's grandparents did a better job with their grandson than they had done with their girl. Learning from experience they refused to be permissive, demanded good behavior and let the consequences be Steve's, not theirs. Steve responded to this more structured and therefore more supportive environment with less anxiety, less hostility and less stress. He stopped smoking pot and went to school and began getting decent grades. As he relaxed he gradually began to change his ways if not his looks. He even modified his attitude toward his mother a bit.

In most cases where adolescents get out of control or on drugs, the grandparents are unable to have a direct role. Still, grandparents can help, if nothing else, by standing firm on disapproval of drug use and other self-defeating behavior.

Grandparent's Approval

Adolescents need the approval of their elders. When they get into serious trouble they certainly need their grandparent's help and support:

Angela

The Associated Press reported a story about four young people who burned a church founded by free slaves. They were caught, fined and had to pay to rebuild the church. The judge insisted that they personally apologize. Nineteen-year-old Angela, head bowed, said to the congregation, "What we did was still wrong. And I am sorry." The congregation gave the young people a round of applause as they left the church. Angela's grandfather listened from the church doorway and afterwards said he was proud of her courage in taking responsibility for her actions. His being there was a statement and his brief words of praise offered her a way out, a way to accept good values, structure and responsibility. Fortunately few grandparents have to offer support under such circumstances, but in smaller ways most of us can and do offer such support.

Being an involved grandparent with an adolescent may not be easy. Each of us has different pulls in life. Many grandparents have jobs or interests which make it difficult to give much time to the grandchildren, especially to teenagers who seem so uninterested in them — so wound up with their own lives. But a stitch in time saves nine. Do what you can to help prevent trouble. Touch base with your grandchildren periodically. Being interested in their life, their friends and their plans, validates their importance.

Jim and Marge

Jim and Marge's three boys joined a rock band while they were in high school. The band played "gigs" at dances or night clubs. Jim and Marge would go to a few (not often) of their performances, have a beer and dance too. The impact was impressive. It made them "good guys" in the eyes of the boys' friends. Few grandparents are likely to go to gigs, but by accepting what they can of modern "music" they can reduce the gap between the young and the elder generation. The younger generation is entitled to it's tastes. Many grandparents today can remember the negative reactions they received from the elder generation to some of their dances whey they were young.

Favors

An occasional favor becomes more important if it responds to the teenager's need at the time, more than if you simply give them something out of the blue. Volunteer to give them a ride to a friend's house if their folks are too busy. Have them stay at your house when mother and father go on a business trip. Root for them at their ball game. Attend family celebrations and the grandchildren's birthdays. If you can't, at least give a call and talk with them. Send letters and cards. Such personal touches offer recognition and support. A hug and a smile often accomplish more than a lecture.

It helps to share the adolescent's enthusiasm and wonder about life. It helps to recognize their need to experiment. This doesn't mean that you should try to act like them, dress like them or talk like them. You are a good model the way you are, so hang onto both your values and your image. But you can appreciate the kids and indirectly share the good feelings of being young while you offer a solid consistent presence for them to lean on, learn from and, along with the parents, be used as a baseline when they look at the world outside of the family. Your value to them is greater than it may appear. Their reward to you of often unsaid respect, of liking and enjoying you, and of depending on your love and wisdom, makes all your efforts worthwhile.

6 PARENTING IS FOREVER!
Parenting Your Adult Children

About the oldest occupation of mankind, and to many the most satisfying, is parenting. Grandparents have experienced the joys and sorrows of parenting: the joy of conceiving, the ecstasy of a new baby, the feeling of dismay and anger when the toddler gets hurt and the pride and sorrow of the first day of kindergarten. Even the most even-tempered parents experience the emotional roller coaster ride that goes with parenting. This naturally guilt-tinged trip has rewards beyond comparison. Yet it can create an anxiety-ridden life with confusion, self-doubt, and for some a sense of hopelessness. It hasn't helped that society reduced the status of parents and the family during the last half of the 20th century as the increasing demand for parental perfection met head-on with the conflicting babble of so-called experts. Indeed, although most parents suffered the pangs of separation some parents felt almost overwhelming relief when their children finally grew up and left.

ESCAPE?

When the children left we faced the problem of separation. This was often aggravated by geographical migration in the search for jobs which stressed American families and frequently shattered family networks. As distance made it harder for families to get together, air travel made it more expensive. Still, the end result hasn't diminished the historical truism that parenting is forever. Most parents who planned to retire and play when the children went away, found that life was not that simple. One does not escape from the most significant and lasting product of one's life — the child. Other important endeavors seem to lose some of their relative significance when compared to your children. But what if your children want too much from you?

They Want Too Much!

Sometimes it seems that adult-children or their spouses don't appreciate the work and effort expended by their parents. Growing up in affluence, sometimes in isolation from much real contact with their working parents, gave them little real awareness of work. Many children today don't know what their parents really do for a living. They leave for "somewhere" in the morning and come back in the evening. Nor do many adult-children appreciate how easy they had it during their childhood. They assumed that what they saw, what they experienced was normal. Life without television? Impossible! The results of affluence can lead to problems, as it did for Earl and Marvin.

Earl

Nine-year-old Earl wasn't doing too well in public school. His parents decided not to take the trip to Europe they had wanted so they could afford to send him to Ford Country Day School, an expensive private school. After Earl had been there a few weeks he asked his father, "Dad, how come we don't have a Mercedes?" The cars most parents used to take their children to school were mostly Mercedes, Rolls Royces, or Cadillacs; these did outclass the old Chevrolet Earl's mother used to take him to school. He didn't understand that his parents had more limited means than most of his schoolmates' families or that his parents had really sacrificed to give him a better education.

Marvin

The mother of Marvin, one of Earl's classmates, taught piano forty hours a week to be able to afford to send him to Ford Country Day School. Marvin grew up to become a successful lawyer. He was shocked when his mother got angry because he asked her to take his two boys, ten and twelve-year-old Arnold and Samuel, for a month while he and his wife toured Europe. Marvin's mother was probably also a little jealous. She and her husband had never been able to afford a trip to Europe and didn't think it fair to baby sit for free while the son she slaved over lived the "good life." Was she justified in her anger?

If our adult-children grew up with an unrealistic or unfair view of life we need to keep in mind our role in shaping that attitude. Perhaps we were too permissive and didn't demand enough of them. They probably do not realize how hard we worked or the sacrifices we made. When we grew up and wanted a ride to school on a rainy day, many of us were regaled with the stories from our parents or grand-parents, "When I was your age I used to walk two miles in the snow to get to school." Then we would be told to get our raincoat on and start walking. Did we do that with *our* now adult-children? How many of us invited our parents to go to Europe with us if we went?

Earl, Again

When Earl graduated from private school he asked his parents to send him to Europe. Most of his classmates were going — a sort of reward for finishing high school. Earl's mother told him, "Your father and I have never been to Europe. If you want to go, fine. But you will have to earn the money yourself." Earl accepted that reality, worked a year and saved enough to go to Europe.

It is not too late to be honest and realistic with your adult-children now. Ask them why you should take care of the grandchildren free while they play. Maybe they should take you and the children with them? You have to balance your values and needs with the needs of your grandchildren and the needs and desires of your adult-children. You don't have to give until it hurts. In fact it really shouldn't hurt at all. Having the grandchildren live with you for a month may be a very rewarding experience for all of you.

One does not easily avoid the primal ancestral force which ties us to our grandchildren. But to answer the pull of our grandchildren we have to deal with their parents, our own adult-children and their spouses. That relationship depends, to a large degree, on how we raised them. Each of us used our own method, our own style of parenting when they were growing up. The question is, will that style work well now that our children are adult, and is it the best to use for our grandchildren? Such questions become even more significant if our adult-children come back to live with us.

Living Together — Living Apart?

People deal with the problems inherent in close family relations in many ways. A few generations ago in New England, economics and custom often led to the son or daughter bringing the new spouse back home to live. The large rambling old farm houses, with six or seven bedrooms added on over time, now outmoded and often abandoned, speak to the economic and social changes which evolved since our grandparent's lifetimes. These stately, two-story clapboards dotting the countryside in Vermont and Maine give mute testimony to the force of change. They also remind us of family needs in evolving society. Now, as then, the nuclear family desires some privacy and autonomy. But when adult-children marry and form their own nuclear family with children, grandparents are still needed. The issues are complex; the basis of human relations and the outcome of human evolution are at stake. Looking at a small segment of evolution we see natural continuing problems of human relationships and autonomy in this arena.

Problems

When a spat occurs between husband and wife, especially in a shaky marriage, the wife may threaten to leave and "go home to mother." The bond between husband and wife becomes less primary than the bond between parent and child. This possibility threatens many marriages. Some jealous spouses insist on 100% commitment with complete exclusion of the spouse's parents. Often such couples move away from their parents, driven by a desire for "non-interference." In some cases this represents the adult-child's desire or need to be free of the domination of his or her own parents.

Getting Along With Your Adult-Children and Their Spouses

Although most of us get along easily with our adult-children and spouses, stresses still occur. They are often hidden because the positive aspects of the relationships outweigh the negative ones. Yet, emotional sore toes distort the attitudes of grandparents, adult-children, spouses and grandchildren toward each other. This can mute the pleasures of family closeness or make the relationship a downright pain. This may explain why some grandparents talk as if they simply want to go do their own thing, almost making a fetish out of avoiding their adult-children and grandchildren. In the chapter on divorce you will see that few really follow through and avoid their distressed adult-children and grandchildren; they get involved anyway when the chips are down. They, and the majority of grandparents who feel the compelling need to keep the family together, have to learn as much as possible about how to get along with their offspring and in-laws.

Separating

One of the first things that must be faced when attempting to get along with your adult-children is that you must separate from them. The intensity and closeness of the parent-child relationship usually equals that of the marriage. For some, the children represent the reason for and the major bond of marriage. But over time the parent/child relationship must change to the parent/adult-child relationship. You have held him close, now let him go. This emotional separation must occur to allow the new adult to live his or her own life.

Turning children out, separating, is rarely easy for us or for them. Four-year-olds worry about leaving home in the future and many of them decide that the solution is to marry Mom or Dad so they can stay forever. Five-year-olds looking forward to kindergarten, ten-year-olds looking forward to junior high and seventeen-year-olds looking forward to college sometimes suffer separation anxieties. The exhilaration of growing up and leaving overcomes the fears and a new adult finally enters the world stage. But that adult is still the child, albeit the adult-child of the parents.

Some parents do find it exceedingly difficult to let their child go. It's not uncommon for parents to tell their little children, "Just stay like you are!" They want to parent forever, still treating their children like little children rather than accept them as the adults they have become. This lack of a healthy emotional separation can lead to family stress.

When you recognize and accept the need for a healthy emotional separation you can then develop new and rewarding relationships with your adult-children, their spouses and their children. Such relationships thrive on diplomacy and recognition of each other's feelings and needs. Friendliness, support and love can increase if you know when to let go, if you will relinquish a lot of the parental power that you had when they were younger, and respect the adult status of the next generation.

Sally

Sally wrote movingly of Mark's graduation, "A mother always has a special sadness in her heart as she watches her youngest step up to receive the college diploma that says the last of her little ones is ready to venture forth into a world that is no longer protective. This mother is no different. As I sat on the hill on that delightful blue-sky day and watched Mark graduate, I knew my years of mothering were closing. . . Dan and I find ourselves back to where we began, only with more space. Just the two of us tending to each other's needs."

Sally hasn't finished however. We continue to parent our children whether we try to or not. Even those who try to withdraw from any contact with their children continue to have an effect. By their lack of interest they deliver a powerful message. Usually not a positive one; neglecting parents offer a poor model and can have a bad effect, even on adult children. Yet, sometimes it's the other way around.

The Power Factor

Some adult-children ignore or avoid their parents because of an uncomfortable relationship. The reasons may not be obvious to the parents, and usually must be understood before a comfortable relationship can be built. One of the more common reasons is misuse of parental power. As we have seen, authoritarian parents overuse power and many of their children do not have the opportunity to develop their own power — to really grow up. Thus, they may be insecure, look for authority figures to direct them, lack initiative and at the same time harbor a deep rebellion against authority — against their parents.

Adult-children need the opportunity to develop their power in healthy ways. They need independence, they should have the opportunity to lead and to make decisions for themselves. Parents should try to respect such decisions even if they aren't always the wisest. Wise parents trying to reestablish good relations may find it useful to ask their adult-children for advice and gratefully follow some of that advice. This increases the adult-child's self respect and enhances his opinion of his parent's intelligence. In turn, it makes it more likely that he will be willing to listen to your viewpoint.

The Power of Guilt

A not uncommon reason that some adult-children avoid their parents is the feeling of guilt. Claudette Wassil-Grimm wrote in *How To Avoid Your Parent's Mistakes When You Raise Your Children*:

"I only recently identified that the predominant feeling I have had toward my own mother was guilt. She left me no room to miss her or talk to her. She always seemed to be hovering over me like a heavy mist, expecting more from me than I could give, so she was perpetually dissatisfied with me. She didn't take care of her own needs. As a result, my siblings and I were all expected to fill the tremendous vacuum in her life. Having a relationship with my mother felt like falling into a bottomless pit.

"The flip side of guilt is expectation. People with excessive expectations cannot simply 'accept the things they cannot change.' My mother often goes on and on about how my brothers have let her down. However her expectations are so unreasonable in the first place that they can't help but let her down. No one could deliver what she expects. I heard a speaker recently who said, 'The most you should expect from anybody is disappointment and then all the rest will be gravy'."

Guilt feelings lead many adult-children to develop "logical" reasons for avoiding close contact with their parents. Not uncommonly the adult-child takes the next step, turns the tables and blames the parent for demanding closer relations; he may even blame the parents for his own problems, an easy way to avoid responsibility for one's own life. Sometimes it *is* overexpectation on the part of the parent. Other times it represents a hidden guilt over feelings buried from childhood. For example, if a child gets angry at mother he feels that he has hurt her with this anger. This makes him feel guilty, so child-like he buries the hurt deeply. But buried doesn't mean gone. Such feelings may have life-time effects.

With or without guilt, adult-children remain acutely sensitive to their parent's feelings of approval or disapproval. Most often words needn't be said. Living with each other for two decades of life make both parent and child well aware of each other's values, moods and reactions. The adult-child has the freedom to make his or her own decisions, but these decisions are often modified by an awareness of the parent's attitudes. Autonomy and free choice balance with parentally induced values. Sometimes the parent's feelings and values have more of an effect on the adult-child now than it did when his choices were influenced by the rebellion and immaturity of youth.

Smothering

As we saw earlier, rational-authoritative parenting produces the most competent, socially responsible children. The commitment to the child represents unselfish love. But the issue of unselfishness requires definition. Many parents, if it comes down to it, would give their lives for their children. But some love so intensely that it over-powers the child. A few love so much that they smother the child with excessive attention, gifts and demands but don't allow the child the freedom to be himself. Some, for example, continue economic sup-port when the adult-child does nothing — robbing him of the need to make his own living.

Adults may be smothered by excessive parental demands for time and attention. Sensible grandparents recognize that their adult-child, and even the grandchildren, face many demands on their time and energy. If the parent adds to these demands by insisting on more time and attention than can be comfortably given, the visits may become more stressful than fun. Concentrate on making your time with them interesting, relaxing and rewarding. Avoid complaining. Even with your own adult-children, honey does catch more flies than vinegar. But be aware that too much honey, too much demanding love, can also create problems. Note that some parents become jealous of their adult-child's spouse because they have not been able to let go emotionally. Often this becomes the source of the common mother-in-law problems that effect so many marriages.

MOTHER-IN-LAW PROBLEMS

The mother-in-law problem is a common barrier to the easy acceptance of grandparents into the lives of their adult-children and grandchildren. The source of continuing jokes and stories, strained relations with the in-laws occur in many families. Why mother-in-law rather than father-in-law? Does this represent another facet of preju-dice against women? The answer probably lies in biology, in the uterus. Nothing ever replaces the miraculous feeling of a baby in the uterus or the intense maternal-infant bonding in the first few months of life. Also, most grandmothers of today stayed at home mothering full-time when their children were little. A mother normally looks on her child as part of herself. Identification can be so complete that a mother thinks nothing of enthusiastically telling father about their Susie, "We went to the potty today!" The biological and emotional identification of mothers with their children remains an evolutionary constant which helps assure the survival of the species — but which can create problems for a son-in-law or daughter-in-law.

Fathers traditionally don't bond as thoroughly to their children as do mothers. Men are frequently faulted by women in courtship and marriage because they do not invest as much in interpersonal relations as do women. Little boys aggressively explore more than little girls who routinely invest more effort in interpersonal relations. Evolution most likely hung on to this characteristic because the male must be more aggressive to defend the family. Too close a bond might make leaving to chase mastodons or fight invading tribes too difficult. Men historically have to be tough. In any case, most men find separation easier to deal with than women. As grandparents, men usually distance themselves more from the grandchildren than do grandmothers. However the sweeping changes facing our grandchildren speak to the need for grandfathers to become far more involved than in the past. Meanwhile, as fathers, they can help their wives with support, love and understanding as they adapt to the "loss" of their children.

Both mothers and fathers experience some difficulty when their children leave the nest. Many mothers shed silent tears when their children went off to kindergarten that first day — although admittedly some celebrated. A popular old movie, "*Take Her, She's Mine*," parodied the problems fathers have letting their girls go in marriage. Emotionally few of us ever separate all the way. Nor should we. Our children, our flesh and blood, our investment of "the best years of our lives" remains a prime bond not to be denied. But these close ties are perceived by current society as being threatening to the marriage bonds between your child and his or her spouse. Even in societies where the dominance of the matriarchal grandmother remains intact and accepted, some mothers-in-law make life miserable for their daughters-in-law. The sanctity of marriage seems to conflict with the sanctity of the parent-child relationship.

All sorts of horror stories exist about domineering mothers-in-law or ungrateful, selfish daughters-in-law. Sons should honor their mothers, and if they don't they suffer a huge guilt trip. And wives should respect their mothers-in-law and visa versa. If they don't it creates all sorts of problems. Certainly it did for Molly, a rather rigid mother of four happily growing girls. She felt depressed after each vacation visit with her husband's parents.

Molly

After years of stewing about how her mother-in-law treated her, Molly decided not to go on the usual family summer vacation with them. She wrote Janice, her mother-in-law, "John and I have been married eleven years, and you have never accepted me. You always criticize the way I raise my children, the way I dress, and you told me I don't belong with your family. So John will join you this summer while the children and I will go to visit my mom."

Janice wrote back, ". . .I am 69, so this is probably one of the last years I will be around to see my grandchildren. If I criticized it was to help you become a better wife and mother. I do not know of any custom of society which indicates honor thy children. Instead, the old law is honor thy mother.

"You have never acknowledged me as your mother-in-law. You haven't taught your children social graces. It is natural for children to wet their bed until they are shamed. It is your responsibility to shame them and you haven't. Your house is a mess. I brought you all sorts of things, yet you make nasty remarks instead of thanking me. I will not put up with disrespect!"

The letters increased the hard feelings. Accusations and counter accusations accomplish little. Diplomacy was needed as well as plain speech. This often comes hard for a parent who believes that her child married beneath his station. Often the adult-child's mother feels she has really lost her child when he marries. Therein lies one key. No longer is he a child and no longer can the parent control him or her. Parental power must decrease or the child cannot become an independent adult. It takes a sensible and mature grandparent to handle such feelings and not let them interfere with the relationship with the grandchildren. *This requires the realization that by losing the child you gain an adult-child who is both friend and family.*

Mothers-in-Law Are Not All That Bad!

Stacey

"What do you want to do when you grow up Stacey?" her pediatrician asked. "I want to be a mommy and when the baby comes out I want Grandma there!" replied the happy, charming and bright-eyed four-year-old. When asked to draw a picture of her family Stacey put her mother, father and grandmother on one level and drew herself in below.

Stacey's type of extended family has decreased over the last decades even though Stacey recognizes the need and the importance of having grandma around. Stacey was born back East and her mother talked her father into moving to California to be near Stacey's remaining widowed grandmother. When the family first arrived they stayed with Stacey's grandmother temporarily. This temporary stay has extended now for four years. Stacey's dad, who wasn't exposed to grandparents when he grew up, was uncomfortable at first living with his mother-in-law. Now, when he tells friends that he and his family live with his mother-in-law he has become used to their mouths dropping open and incredulously saying, "You live with your mother-in-law? I could never live with mine!"

"Well, yours must be different than mine. We have no problems." replies Stacey's dad.

Before they moved in, Stacey's grandmother had entertained the idea of selling the house as it was too big for her alone. But after a month she suggested that they might as well stay and it would be more economical for all of them. Her list of "understandings", that Stacey's mom would shop for the groceries and do most of the cooking, and that she wouldn't baby sit Stacey full time, had one other provision:

"Every six months we will meet and discuss any problems and decide whether we want to continue this arrangement." They met twice, had no problems, and haven't met officially since.

Stacey is in part time day care. Her mother didn't want to take advantage of Grandma and stick her with full time care of her child. Stacey regards Grandma as a full time participant in her life. Mother and father, at first, found that they felt uncomfortable having any argument in the house because Grandma might hear them. Over the past few years they realized that most "arguments" were discussions that involved all four in the home, so they now talk openly. Grandmother gives her opinion if asked, otherwise tends to just listen. The entire family goes on vacations together. Mom and Dad get away together a few days a year to assert their privacy. However Dad relates to his mother-in-law so well now that he doesn't feel any great need to get away. They all feel fortunate that they can keep the extended family together and help each other.

THE HEAVY HAND OF THE PAST

Even if you avoid being heavy-handed with your adult-child and even if you try to avoid using guilt, the past can catch up with you. This is especially true if competition between the parents for the child's affection took place long ago — or takes place now. Usually this results from a lack of teamwork between parents, allowing the child to take over and manipulate them in an unhealthy way. Often this leads to stress during the child's growth which may resurface, especially if the adult-child moves in with the parents again. Chronic chaos may result, as it did for Marisa and her parents.

Marisa

Marisa's mother and father moved to a suburb of Portland when Mr. Brent retired after 30 years as a machinist at the Boeing factory in Seattle. Marisa and her one-year-old Becky moved in with them. As a single working mother who had never married, Marisa had little choice. Prior to the move Marisa had gotten along fairly well with her mother although she hadn't respected her. "Mom used to bribe us kids to make us mind. Even when she punished us it was no big deal — we put up with it and just shrugged our shoulders and did what we wanted anyway. I guess we never respected her, but she was really nice. My dad was tough and I didn't like him."

Things changed when Marisa and Becky moved in. Marisa had always rebelled against her mother, but now she began to really dislike her mother and like her dad more. Her mother disagreed with Marisa's discipline and if Becky was punished, grandmother would pick her up and comfort her. Grandfather agreed with Marisa's discipline and the way she handled Becky. After a few months a pattern emerged. Almost whatever Marisa did, her mother criticized her while her father stepped in and defended her. Mother became even more angry at these times, finally to the point that she threatened to leave. Marisa laughed and threw her head back in a body language challenge to "go ahead!"

During Becky's two-year check-up Marisa complained to her pediatrician, Dr. Harvey, about the stress at home saying she couldn't wait to move out but couldn't afford to. She felt bad about fighting with her mother and said she was resolving not to call her a "damned bitch" anymore even if she just said it under her breath.

Marisa's problems encompassed many issues. First her mother's permissive child rearing probably contributed to Marisa's unwed pregnancy as Marisa tended to take impulsive actions without regard for the consequences. Like many permissively raised adult-children she retained an underlying anxiety yet wanted limits and security. This she found from her father, and she appreciated it more now that she was an adult. He listened to her, respected her and supported her. His demands for more responsible behavior when she was a child finally made sense to Marisa.

Permissive grandmothering interfered with Marisa's attempts to control Becky. Grandmother's permissive instincts ran counter to Marisa's decision to be a more authoritative parent. The conflict gradually resulted in Marisa and her mother really disliking each other. Grandmother's reaction would probably not have been so negative if her husband hadn't become openly involved on Marisa's side. He, understandably, had objected in the past to permissive childrearing. Now that Marisa was an adult and refused to raise Becky permissively, the stage was set for family conflict.

Grandmother saw herself the victim of collusion between her husband and her daughter. Her husband's perceived loyalty switch created bitterness and resentment leading to the threat to leave — but there was no place to go. So she took her anger out on Marisa, finding fault with everything she did, claiming that Marisa was ruining her granddaughter. Her husband became more and more frustrated but found that the only way to deal with the situation was to ignore his wife. This made her so angry that the strain had become almost intolerable for the family.

Dr. Harvey, after sorting out the story, advised Marisa to first see if she couldn't get her dad to support her mother on as many issues as possible — even when he didn't fully agree with her stand on raising their granddaughter. The father was also urged to get his wife out of the house for evenings or short vacation trips where they could enjoy each other. Marisa's feelings of guilt about displacing her mother led her to begin socializing, going to church, getting to know other people, and going away some weekends and evenings.

Before things could settle down Marisa had to change her negative attitude toward her mother. Dr. Harvey reminded her to really express her thanks to her mother for her support, for taking Becky and her in. As the tensions subsided a bit Marisa studied a book on child rearing, recommended by the pediatrician. She then offered it to her mother saying that Dr. Harvey thought it might help the two of them become more of a team in raising Becky. Over time the stress subsided and Marisa was able to go to college and prepare for a better paying job and a more independent future. She and mother could finally become friends.

FRIENDSHIP

While the relationship between a parent and her adult-child is more than a friendship, there is no reason why friendship cannot be one pillar of the relationship. We often treat our friends differently than we treat our children. In part, this is because we do not feel as responsible for the actions of our friends as we do for the actions of our children. So we are more cautious about how we use our power on our friends. Generally we are friends because we respect and like each other. The same attitude goes a long way towards developing good relations with our adult-children. Perhaps the best reward we can offer friends and our adult-children is respect. And if we don't respect them it becomes harder to like them.

Motivating Change

Some adult-children really act like little children in so many ways that it becomes hard to respect them. Yet as parents we usually love them anyway. To be able to help them develop adult responsibility and behavior, start by finding something about them to respect. Everyone has some redeeming qualities. The best way to make a person receptive to change is to offer respect at the same time you suggest change. Find some characteristic in your adult-child worthy of respect and show that respect in the way you treat him and talk to him. As a parent you probably understand his personality and can choose a method that will motivate him to develop some responsible behavior. Of course, you may have already tried and failed. Sometimes it is hard to understand what makes a particular child tick. In such cases it may be helpful to seek professional help and counseling before making any further efforts to help him grow up. Sometimes it requires giving him space, leaving him alone, allowing him to develop on his own.

In evaluating one's feelings toward an adult-child, it remains important to not expect perfection. We don't expect children to be perfect — at least we don't if we are rational. Few of us reach perfection, even with the experience of decades of living under our belts. So mistakes are made, by us, by our adult-children and by our grandchildren. When mistakes are made the important lesson most grandparents have learned from experience is not to overreact or criticize. Natural consequences usually punish enough and motivate the child to avoid similar problems in the future. For example, if your adult-child is arrested by the police for speeding and drunk driving, the suspension of his driving permit usually makes the point. So does the parent's acceptance of the justice of the punishment by the courts by saying calmly, "Well, that's what happens."

Little is accomplished by adding parental criticism. Your adult-children already know your values and opinions. We all hate to have salt rubbed into our wounds. Parental criticism tends to dilute the lesson of natural consequences and draws attention to the person who criticized rather than to correcting the misbehavior. Let the facts speak for themselves. Bite your tongue and the outcome may be better.

WHAT ADULT-CHILDREN WANT FROM THEIR PARENTS

1. Your respect for their adult status.
2. Your acceptance of their right to have their own feelings and viewpoints.
3. Your understanding and empathy.
4. Your encouragement and belief in their abilities.
5. Your viewpoint and advice when asked for.
6. Your freely given support and help when you can afford it.
7. Your living up to your own values.
8. Your attempt to be as self sufficient and independent as possible.
9. Your comfortable and dignified acceptance of their help if needed.
10. Your relaxed, honest and open communication with them.
11. Your openly expressed love for them.
12. Your love, interest and appreciation of your grandchildren.
13. Your understanding and acceptance of their spouse.
14. Your help with the grandchildren.

WHAT ADULT-CHILDREN WANT
FROM THEIR PARENTS

One of our greatest needs as adults (or as children) is to be understood by our parents. Understanding leads to the approval we want and need. Empathy gives us a sense of security, lack of empathy distances people. Try to accept and understand your adult-child's emotional responses rather than simply judging or reacting to them. Most grandparents have learned not to react to anger with counter-anger or to let depression turn them off. We can nurture our adult children with empathy, with mature behavior which allows them to openly ventilate emotions with us. Lending a sympathetic ear allows mature grandparents to quietly and effectively offer their viewpoints at appropriate times. When you refrain from criticism and actively listen, you may be able to subtly guide the conversation and make it more likely that your adult-child will hear you and make rational decisions.

By respecting and accepting the decisions they make, you help your "kids" build autonomy. This encourages their self-confidence and helps them become competent. It sets the stage so your child can, in turn, accept and respect you and maybe even take some of your advice without feeling that his status as an adult is threatened.

Cheryl, a bright eyed grandmother, knew that her children needed respect and understanding. She learned how to offer this — she had learned by undergoing the ultimate experience of successfully raising children. She found that this matured her more than any other experience in life. It also helped her develop her basic philosophy of dealing with people, "Do unto others as you would have them do unto you," and enabled her to offer some sensible advice. Her basic respect for people showed when she told us how she related to her family.

Cheryl

"One of the most difficult things about grandparenting is learning to keep quiet. Much of our style of raising our children was based on our own need for structure, to keep the confusion down. Our rules governing behavior — one does not throw food on the floor — were to our minds the only rational way. When our first granddaughter, Erin, was given total choice about what she ate and how she ate it, I had to bite my tongue not to give some 'helpful advice.' Erin is now a very civilized college freshman who is willing to try any new food and has beautiful table manners. Obviously being allowed to 'experience her food' as a child did not warp her — though I am grateful that it was my daughter Louise, not I, who had to clean up after her.

"John, our second son, is raising his children with rules more similar to ours. The interesting thing is that John was the rebel when he was growing up. He was the one who pushed everything to the limits and beyond. I find it much easier to be with his children because they live by the rules. These days I have to work hard at not favoring one family over the other. In the abstract I love them all equally but in the concrete it is difficult to have children visiting who raid the refrigerator whenever they feel like it, and eat and spill snacks wherever they happen to be. I keep reminding myself that Erin turned out well.

"It is much more difficult for me to not offer unsolicited advice to my daughter about her children. I'm sure that my desire not to alienate Mary, my daughter-in-law, makes some of the difference. I never criticize after the fact, but if Mary is telling me about some ongoing problem, she is open to any suggestions I might make. Even then I work hard at not 'laying down the law,' saying this is the right way to handle the situation.

"My husband and I really respect our children and their spouses, and we affirm this by telling them what a good job they are doing as parents. When our children were small Garry's job was to earn the money and I, not he, was involved in the children's lives on a day-to-day basis. We are delighted that in our children's families the daddies are very involved in their children's hands-on care."

Authoritarian grandparents who don't learn to keep quiet and who offer unsolicited advice often find that it creates problems; especially when the grandparent feels critical about the way the adult-child or his or her spouse is raising the grandchild. Linda, an adult-child raised by an authoritarian mother, stewed about her mother's recurrent criticism of three-year-old Jacklyn's behavior. She finally snapped, "Mother, I've had it up to here!" Linda's hand indicated her chin, "I will not spank Jacky like you spanked me. If you don't like it you don't have to come around!"

Grandparenting Diplomacy

Most grandparents learn early on to respect their adult-child's prerogative to raise their own children. It is a very sensitive area from both the parent's and the grandparent's views. Some grandparents, like Greg, found that a diplomatic approach works. After worrying about how his adult daughter, Joyce, didn't discipline her two rowdy boys, he approached the problem by looking for a time when the boys were completely out of control and Joyce was fully exasperated with them.

Greg

Greg handed his daughter a cup of coffee and said, "That must be hard on you, Joyce, to keep from spanking those kids when they act that way. I wish that I had been able to control my temper better when you were that age. I sometimes felt bad after I spanked you and I'm not sure that it did a lot of good. You new generation of parents have the advantage of better education. I've been admiring the way Mrs. Jalice, you know, that young mother who moved next door to us, handles her kids. She just quietly tells them to go to their room and they do! It sure is different than the way I handled you. I would holler and spank and it was always a hassle. I asked her and she said that she had taken a good parenting course."

Grandfather offered an indirect way that his daughter could use without "losing face." A somewhat similar approach was used by Rose, who wanted her granddaughter to take more pride in her appearance.

Rose

Rose's neatness and fashionable dress contrasted acutely with her daughter-in-law's messiness. Betty put most of her energy into community affairs and paid little attention to the housework, her clothes or the way her teenage daughter, Jane, dressed. Betty's sloppy dress habits did not interfere with her success in community politics, her husband's love and admiration for her or the job she did stimulating Jane's academic success. Rose was tempted to comment on Betty's dress habits but, with some effort, wisely restrained herself. Still she wanted to pass on the value of good grooming to her granddaughter.

The chance came when Jane visited for a week before school started. Rose called Betty and offered to help Jane purchase her school clothes. Betty, who was involved in a city council planning session, happily agreed. Rose invested some of her own money as an "early Christmas gift" to supplement the funds Jane was allowed for school clothes. Jane enjoyed the shopping trip with grandmother and was very pleased with the compliments of her family and friends about her fashionable dress.

What Cheryl said bears repeating, "One of the most difficult things about grandparenting is learning to keep quiet." Rose managed to keep quiet and still get her values across to her grandchild without criticism. As a sage said, one picture is worth a thousand words — and one shopping spree is worth a thousand criticisms.

HOW WE FUNCTION

Growing Apart — Growing Together

The emotional and practical bonds between parent and child change as the child grows and develops. Parental powers necessarily decrease, often leaving both parents and their adolescents somewhat uncertain and anxious. The innate feeling of guilt which accompanies the job of parenting leads to self-doubt. We ask, "How good a parent have I been?" Conversely, the teenager asks, "Am I really ready to become an adult?" The instinctive and logical realization that the adult-child must be independent can drive a wedge between parent and teenager which can last into adult life, each drawing apart from the other. Sometimes this is exaggerated by the parent's overreaction to the child's desire for continued dependance. Conversely the parent's difficulty in letting go can make the child feel that he must escape his parents in order to function as an adult. These feelings increase the need to establish separate households, and to physically move far away from bonds which demand too much. Similarly, the parents may seek a completely independent life 'free' of the kids or the grandkids. "I've served my time, done my duty" – many say – "It's time to play." Yet the bond remains, a genetic instinctive basic pull which is rarely thwarted.

Once parents do let go and accept the child as an adult, relationships generally improve. The process may also open up hidden aspects of personality and feelings that children, even those raised by excellent parents, kept to themselves. Sometimes this reflects a need for privacy, sometimes it springs from the experience that expressing certain feelings may cause unexpected or negative parental reactions. One grandmother after having her adult-daughter and granddaughter live with her for a year said, "It's good my daughter is living with us so we can sort of get acquainted. Children often live their own silent lives, unobtrusive, hidden from parents. When they become adults they may comfortably bare this part of their lives."

Healthy emotional separation and mutual respect reduce the need for physical separation between parents and their adult-children. All of them, and the grandchildren, can even live together in the same house enjoying and supporting each other with minimal strain. This relationship may occur quite naturally as it has many times in history and still does in many cultures. However, for many this bond is weakened by problems of communication, territorialism, time and loyalties.

Communication

Communication represents more than just words — it represents the realities of feelings, of actions, of expectations met or unmet. Good communication requires realism in both thought and substance. When the relative powers of the parents and the adult-child balance well, communication becomes easier. However, if the parent tries to overpower the adult-child or if the adult-child rebels against what he perceives to be an ego damaging directive from the parent, communication becomes difficult. It seems easier not to talk about negative feelings. It also is difficult if the demands of the adult-child are too great, frequently the result of permissive child rearing or past overindulgence. All this means that the communication of rational expectations works best when a healthy balance of demand, response and giving exists. Communication is not just words.

Body Language

Sometimes people do not realize that they are communicating negative feelings. They think that if they don't say something, it isn't communicated. But students of communication point out that probably 70% of communication involves body language and tone. One common trap is when we say one thing but underneath it all mean another. Children certainly recognize what a person means before they understand the words. Communicating negative thoughts or attitudes rarely helps situations. Brutal honesty, far from always being admirable, can cause unnecessary hurt. When you do talk with your adult-child, watch your body language. Facial expressions, body tone and movement communicate much of what is being said.

Improving Communication

If you want to communicate well or negotiate, then make it a two-way conversation by responding in an adult way, rather than with an overbearing parental monologue or a childish blowing off of steam. William Summers, M.D., in his book *The House of Marriage*, diagrammed possible responses based on which mode you are in when you communicate: the parental authority state (P), the rational adult state (A) or the instinctive childish state (C).

To be effective, in the adult state, respect the person you talk to and honestly mean what you say. If you communicate respect you are more likely to persuade the person to take the position or action you want. If the parental imprint or the instinctive child portion takes over and you speak dictatorially or childishly, in anger or from hurt, it tends to frazzle the ties that bind. Your adult-child deserves at least as much respect and acceptance as you give your friends — a warm, supportive, trusting attitude. Rarely do people talk "down" from their parental imprint stance to adults they respect or want as friends. We don't patronize, scold, demand or try to feed our ego by demonstrating superiority with our friends. Those who treat friends or their adult-children that way will soon lose that friendship. They may drive adult-children, with the grandchildren, out of their lives.

To get along with our adult-children it helps to recognize what level we function on. We never completely outgrow the childish portion of our psyche. Nor do we outgrow the imprint of our parents, our life as a child or our reaction to the way we were raised. Hopefully though, we reach an adult status where we are able to use our logic and reason more than our instincts and our imprints. Each person has her own particular balance, her own degree of adult self control, often determined by the current stress level. How we balance these parts of our psyche determines our personalities. This balance also determines our effectiveness as grandparents and as the parents of our adult-children as is shown by our ability to communicate. The really good news is that we are not fixed in cement; with maturity we learn and we begin to act differently than we did when we were younger. This growth of wisdom and diplomacy needn't stop at any age. For example, if you critically ask your daughter about your granddaughter's school problems, you probably will get a negative response:

Parent: "Well, how did Jenny do on that math test!"

Adult-Child, upset that Jenny did poorly and feels that you are critical of her performance as a parent, receives your message as a naughty child being scolded and then responds as an angry child: "Mom, leave Jenny alone! I'll handle that!"

This upsets you, so you reply in a critical parent mode (P) responding to the naughty child (C): "If you weren't so easy on Jenny, she might amount to something."

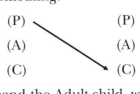

On the other hand the Adult-child, wanting to say (C) "Shut up," instead controls herself and uses her adult diplomat mode and says (A): "Look Mom, I know you are concerned, but really, we are on top of it."

(P)   (P)

(A) ◄——————— (A)

(C)   (C)

Keep in mind that you may have been critical of your adult-child a lot in the past. Therefore, she has reason to feel that whatever you say implies criticism. Recognizing this you might start the conversation differently, with the aim of helping Jenny get a tutor if she needs one. So respond on an adult to adult level: "I'm sorry. I didn't mean to be critical. I was just concerned. When I was in the fifth grade like

Jenny I had a terrible time with math. My grandfather helped me get through it. I don't think that I have the patience, though, to be a tutor myself. Does Jenny need help in math? How did she do on that last test?"

Your adult-daughter still may decide your words hide criticism, but that is less likely than in the foregoing examples. Instead, you have opened the door for adult to adult conversation. When you converse, try to have an objective in mind and steer the conversation toward that goal. For example, you may want to try to dispel your daughter's feeling that you are always critical. Start the conversation with a direct honest statement. Parent: "I wanted to ask how Jenny did on that math test but I often sound so critical, even though I shouldn't, that I hesitated asking you. Did I sound critical this time?"

Daughter: "Well. . . I thought that you were going to be critical."

Parent: "I guess that comes from my being raised by such critical parents myself. I never could please my mother. I guess I sound just like her! I hope we can avoid that sort of relationship in the future. Please tell me when you think I am being too critical — I'll try to do better."

Apology or admission of past errors doesn't mean you are eating crow. Rather it represents an adult way to solve problems. More than that, it says that you trust your adult-child to be fair and respond rationally. You respect her opinion and understand that problems are usually not just one sided. You willingly expose your shortcomings and this offers validation of your daughter's independence and judgment.

Understanding What is Meant

Don't try to put words in someone's mouth or assume that you know what he is thinking. When you aren't sure how he really feels, stay silent and available. Allow him to gather his thoughts. Sometimes you can ask general questions and guide a response which would have been difficult otherwise. Instead of criticizing, steer the conversation and control it by the use of questions and suggestions. If you are uncertain about what he means, try saying it in your words and ask if that is what is meant. Don't try to tell him how he feels. Avoid statements like "You are angry." Instead put it in a different frame, "It seems to me that you are angry. Are you?"

Bad Moods

The ties than bind the parent to the adult-child sometimes do not seem to allow for bad moods. If you happen to call when your adult son had a bad day and couldn't argue with his boss, he may answer the phone with a terse, "What do you want?" This hurts, so instead of saying what you had in mind you impulsively and childishly reply, "I just wanted to remind you to bring back the lawnmower you borrowed." This sets the stage for an unwanted squabble. If, instead, you recognize that he is uptight and let your adult diplomatic guidance system take over, you might say, "Oh, I'm sorry I called at a bad time. I just got a letter from Jeanne but I'll read it to you later if you want." Then be prepared for either his telling you his problems or hanging up with a brief "O.K. Mom, later."

Think before you talk and always try to accentuate the positive. Don't overreact, let the rational adult part of your psyche and brain take over. Don't respond with a frozen structured answer that just reflects the past input of your parents. Subtly offer your values and opinions if the opportunity arises and he seems open to them. Accept your adult-child's right to feel as he does whether you agree or disagree with his stand.

TERRITORY AND TIME

More and more adult-children and their families are moving in to live with Mom and Dad. If the house is large enough, and the people involved mature enough, the rent is cheap enough. If you and your adult-child have outgrown the old parent/child relationship then the tensions of close living will be compensated for by your being able to have your grandchildren live with you. But many grandparents aren't too keen on having their immediate family expand that much. Often, however, economics dictate function as they did in New

England's agricultural economy when the adult-child had to continue to help on the farm. The successful merging of several generations of families in the past offers lessons for today, although the reasons may be different. The current major forces behind closing ranks in the extended family are the high divorce rate, the economic difficulties faced by single parents, and the high cost of housing. Evolution responds to necessity. The basic lesson coming out of history is that extended families can live together successfully.

Living together successfully requires more diplomacy, tact and more awareness of each other's needs than usually occurs in an isolated nuclear family. Yet even in isolated nuclear families everyone needs space of their own. Tacit recognition of a person's place at the family table, and certain chairs or couches which "belong" to certain individuals, are ways of respecting territorial boundaries. The establishment of such boundaries and the comfortable sharing of space should be established early on in a family, especially when the family closes ranks and all live together in the same house. A meeting of all family members to discuss each person's needs for territory, and time alone, helps avoid tensions.

Time alone is a precious essential. Most people need time for themselves, unbothered by the presence of others. Winston Churchill spent a half hour each day sitting in a chair away from the house and thinking whatever a genius thinks. A wise pediatrician said that time alone should start when a baby is around nine months old — he should learn to either nap in the crib or contemplate his navel for a couple of hours a day, leaving Mother to do her own thing. Sometimes the time alone can be scheduled. Other times retiring to one's room or going for a walk suffices. We should respect the need for silence as well as the need for companionship.

HOUSEHOLD TASKS

Sharing of household tasks is another aspect of togetherness for the extended family to consider. Extra people make extra work.

Sometimes a formal arrangement isn't needed. Other times newcomers would be better off asking Mom if she wants them to help cook, wash dishes, vacuum or shop for the family or for their portion of the family. The effect of outside jobs and the fatigue grandmothers and grandfathers often feel after a day of baby-sitting a toddler should be factored into the division of labor. Some grandparents and some adult-children demand rigid standards of cleanliness and orderliness. With toddlers and older children around such order becomes hard to keep. This should be openly discussed early on and agreements made about, for example, which rooms the children will be allowed to play in and mess up. Decisions about the division of labor and territory help minimize conflicts over each person's jobs. Flexibility rather than rigid scheduling usually works best. This assumes proper motivation and no shirking of responsibility on anyone's part.

FINANCES

Economic costs exist and must be faced. More often than not the single parent moves in partly because she cannot afford to live alone and support herself and her child. Married couples who move in usually try to save enough for a down payment on their own home. Many grandparents are well able to afford the extra cost. However, people usually feel better when they pay their own way, or at least part of their own way. How much is paid depends to a degree on the financial status of both the grandparents and their adult-children — but even if they are wealthy it makes sense to agree on at least a token payment in cash or labor. Well-off parents contribute best in an indirect manner with gifts on birthdays or holidays. Adult-children whose parents are economically on thin ice may use this technique in reverse or pay real market prices for rent and food.

TRAPS, TRIGGERS AND SOLUTIONS

Many traps exist. Parents used to treating their child like a child may create problems if they try to treat their now adult-child like a child. The adult-child often finds herself responding like a child rather than like an adult. Mixed loyalties may strain the bond between a man and wife moving in with the in-laws. Overexpectations may set the stage for conflict. If the adult-child's mother did the laundry for him when he was a teenager, then he may expect the same service now. Disagreements are bound to occur, but if they are balanced by affection and good listening skills, they needn't become major conflicts.

Some people harbor resentment for years and seize on any current problem to air their anger. Learn to stick to current problems. Consider the family a team and involve everyone in decision-making. Consider everyone's views and encourage them to speak up by listening respectfully. The evolution of modern society makes everybody more dependent on everybody else than in the past. Study of successful models shows that open communication up and down the hierarchy is one key to successful family functioning. Anticipating the needs and problems of others allows the family to plan solutions before problems reach the crisis stage. Teamwork and consensus, rather than competition, becomes the key. We learn, we adapt, we evolve — and our family grows and develops together.

7   GRANDPARENTS AND DIVORCE

Divorce, even when it doesn't tear at the heart, leaves people very sensitized. The issues causing or created by divorce involve a wide spectrum of emotions. The range of problems and personalities makes one hesitate to offer advice in a book. In this chapter, you will read about some people, problems, statistics and the results stemming from divorce which are foreign to many of us. Unfortunately the problems are well known to a lot of children of divorce. These children, especially, need and benefit from their grandparent's support and love. This support can be more effective if you become aware of some of the many difficulties which your grandchildren may face. It also helps to become aware of pitfalls in the relationships between grandparents, parents, stepparents and the grandchildren. So if your grandchildren's parents are divorced or considering divorce, take a deep breath and read on.

First be reassured that the traditional nuclear family is here to stay. So says researcher Colleen Leahy Johnson reporting her research in *Ex Familia,* a book about how grandparents, parents, and children adjust to divorce. She points out that while America has the highest divorce rate it also has the highest marriage rate. The nuclear family of mother-father-child still meets the needs of individuals better than other arrangements. It functions as the basis for personal identity and offers a deep meaning for life. Yet the number of divorces and the accompanying problems are astoundingly high. So are the problems which follow for the parents and children in single-parent families or, in remarriage, for the stepparents, stepchildren and children. Some of these problems spill over into the lives of the grandparents.

The results of divorce, indelibly stamped on the children of divorce, are being measured by scientists. These measurements reveal more problems impacting the children than many had expected. An attitude once existed that divorce is primarily the problem of the husband and wife. The child was perceived to be less affected than the adults. But divorce disintegrates the structure of the world of children. The family splits asunder — but warnings precede the split.

In many divorces the problems which lead to the divorce create as much trouble as the divorce itself. Studies demonstrate that 10 years before the divorce occurs, children in families with conflicts which will lead to divorce behave differently than children in families which don't divorce later. Boys especially become aggressive, impulsive and out of control. Girls in families that will divorce later get along poorly with other children, and are more selfish and jealous. Significantly, if the parents didn't fight much the children appear to have fewer problems both before and after divorce. These could be described as more civilized families with more "civilized" divorces.

Whether most of the child's problems were created by family conflict before divorce or by the results of divorce may not be terribly pertinent to the grandparents. A lot of these children need the stability of grandparents well before divorce occurs. However the physical separation of divorce triggers a series of reactions; first upset, followed by apathy and depression and finally a decreased interest in the parent. Grandparents involving themselves with the child can help reduce the marked anxiety and insecurity which occurs.

DIVORCE FROM THE CHILD'S STANDPOINT

Adults need to know how children feel about divorce. Grandparents especially should be aware of the experiences and the depth and variety of feelings their grandchildren can harbor. Only about ten percent of the children seem to favor their parent's divorce. Most feel only abandonment and insecurity. They feel that one or both of the parents are unfaithful to the other and therefore not dependable for the child. Yet the child's need for faithful and dependable parents requires him to *try* to believe in his parents. As we will see, out of the child's need for faithful and dependable parent figures comes an opportunity for grandparents to step in and fill the gap.

The Guilty One

The turmoil created by divorce creates significant short and long term problems as well as sleeper effects that continue to cause damage even after the child becomes an adult. One problem facing many children of divorce is their sense of guilt. Some kids feel that they are responsible for the separation. Preschoolers who have been naughty, and what preschooler hasn't, may feel that this is why the parent left. One small boy forgot to deliver a note from one parent to the other and blamed himself for this, thinking that it caused the divorce. The normal wish of the four-year-old to marry Mother (to ensure his place in the family when he grows up) suddenly seems to come true. School age children routinely try to play one parent against the other in order to get their way. Even at this age they may not have yet emotionally given up the idea of marriage to one or the other parent. After divorce the child is left with Mother who, in her loneliness, will sometimes take the child to bed with her. This increases the child's feeling that his desires or attempted manipulations caused the divorce.

Occasionally the parent actually believes the child caused the divorce. This happens a lot when a child is developmentally disabled, retarded or handicapped. It can also result from the school age child playing Mother and Father against each other. The child finds it easy to manipulate his parents when major differences exist between the parent's attitudes about discipline. Other times, quite blameless newborns take the rap. *The Motherhood Report*, by Louis and Margolies, contained the following admission by a mother, "I have never been able to warm up to this child. I guess I blame him for my divorce because when he was born that's when things started getting really bad between me and my husband. . . I know there are times I punish him for things one of the others is doing, but I can't help it."

A small number of children face the problem that their mother simply does not like them. Genetic personality differences explain some cases — why some children differ so much from Mother. Or conversely, the child may remind Mother of herself and she doesn't like herself. Or he may be the image of the errant father or a very disliked relative.

Another and perhaps more important problem has to do with Mother's love. *The Motherhood Report* found that "Both single mothers who felt their children would be better off if they had a father living with them and married mothers who felt their husbands were not supportive were less able to love their children and more likely to humiliate and criticize them unfavorably." It's not easy to offer security and love when you don't receive any yourself. Single parents have the almost impossible task of sustaining the home, earning an adequate income, having some social life and caring for the child. Here obvious opportunities exist for grandparents to parent their single adult-child who, almost above all, needs the love and support so she can pass it on to her children.

Abandonment

The personal sorrows in the preschool age center around a fear of abandonment. One parent left. If one parent disappeared, so may the other. Then, when mother has to go to work, he is "abandoned" for the day in day care. The resulting fear, anger and anxiety may cause sleeplessness and hostility. The child's anger combined with feelings of rejection, guilt, worthlessness and yet loyalty to one or both parents, creates confusion and anxiety.

School and Divorce

School work often worsens. Children worry about their parents while in class, rather than really listen or study. C.E. Spangler wrote the following letter to the editor of the Wall Street Journal on March 13 1989, "I have been fortunate in creating security in my adult life and returning to school, to find that subjects that baffled and terrified me as a child are now much more easily comprehended. Childhood anxieties that interfered with my ability to learn were not unrelated to my parents' bitter and protracted divorce and child-custody battles, late child-support payments or visits to our house by the sheriff threatening my mother, working two jobs, with arrest for bounced grocery checks.

"Education begins in the home; the school system is at best a helping hand. The brightest of children may fail to shine on the most standardized tests when they wake up every morning to an empty house of tears and disintegrated values."

Boys long for their father and are sometimes concerned that father will remarry and have another boy and abandon the first son. Sometimes this happens. Few of us comprehend such inhuman, luckily rare, action by a divorced parent and his new wife. Yet some children, like Tony, experienced this.

Tony

Tony grew up in a small town in Maryland. He beat his children if they didn't do well in school. His children *had* to do well because it was necessary for him to prove that they could be as good as Tony's stepbrothers. When Tony's parents divorced, he was the youngest of three boys. Tony's dad kept the boys and remarried a woman with two children and they had two more together. People who visited the home were often amazed to find mother and father and four children eating with the guests in the dining room while Tony, and his two brothers by father's first marriage, ate in the kitchen with the servants. When Tony and his brothers reached age 14, they were turned out of the home to become apprentices in a trade. The stepmother's children were sent to exclusive private schools. Some boys are replaceable.

PAWNS IN THE FIGHT

From the age of 8 to 12 children often take sides. They can become almost pathologically angry at the errant father (or mother) who left, and excessively loyal to the hurt mother left behind. Sometimes they are put in the position of spying on a parent. Other times they are equally angry at Mother for, as the child sees it, making Father leave or visa versa. Sometimes they become pawns, used by each parent to hurt the other. This was the case with Ron and Sam Jolsen.

Ron and Sam

Jim and Mary Jolsen, both thirtyish, well dressed and solemn sat across the desk from the children's pediatrician, Dr. Rantz. They were there to talk about Jim's two boys, Ron age eleven and Sam age nine. Jim had divorced Rena, the boys mother, two years before after falling in love with Mary. Rena was still furious, especially about the court ordered visiting rights Jim had won and about the court ordered child support he was always late in paying. Dr. Rantz had heard her side of the story more often than he wanted. Deep dark eyes flashing, she tensely and recurrently complained about the lack of care she said the children got when visiting their father. She claimed that the boys didn't like to visit the dad because his new wife was a slob and ignored them. She hated Jim with a passion and quizzed the boys each time they came back from a visit to their Dad and "That woman!"

Both Ron and Sam exhibited symptoms of stress: poor grades in school, difficulty going to sleep, and Ron was in trouble for leaving school early and going home without permission. Jim and Mary were attempting to get custody. "This time," Jim announced smugly, "we have her! Listen to this tape. I recorded it the last time I brought the boys home. She was screaming at me through the door. I told the boys she was crazy. This proves it!" He pressed the play button on the recorder and sat rigidly as the tape began to play.

Jim's voice started after the doorbell rang. As the door squeaked open he said, "Ron and Sam are getting their stuff out of the car. They didn't want to come home but Mary and I have to go to a party this evening and . . ." His voice was cut off by a shrill, "You bastard! You don't care about the boys. What did you have them doing all day? Watching television? Its no wonder they have trouble in school. Get out of here!"

Jim loudly interrupted, "I don't blame them for not wanting to come home. You're trying to turn them against me . . ." His voice was drowned out by the slamming of the door. His steps sounded going down the stairs and in the recording the boys could be heard quietly talking as they started up the stairs. The door squeaked open and Rena shouted, "Ron, Sam, come in here this instant. Look, you are both filthy dirty. You poor dears, you look so unhappy. I'll bet you were bored to death over there." As the boys were heard walking by their dad they both mumbled good-by and Jim's voice could be heard muttering, "That bitch!"

Dr. Rantz vainly counseled all the adults involved in "the mess" to stop using the children as pawns in their fight and to spare them exposure to the adult's quarrels. This distorted image of "normal" adult behavior will most likely effect the boys for all of their lives.

THE ADVISOR

Children can also be thrust into the role of parental adviser and helper to a harassed mother who needs someone to depend on for advice but has only the child. Some divorced mothers try to reverse their role with their daughter and try to become dependent on the child by demand and exploitation. For many mothers the combination of powerlessness, grief, loneliness and anxiety overwhelms them and, in turn, overwhelms the child. Such stress leads to lying, psychosomatic stomach aches and headaches, truancy and antisocial behavior. Yet their need for an ideal father who loves and supports them may also lead to fantasizing about an absent dad and giving him unrealistic qualities. This then creates conflict with Mother and leads to further disillusionment when the child sees Dad.

DISTRUST

It surprises some researchers that the distrust of people created by divorce lasts so long. Adults who experienced divorce as children tend to have reduced faith in interpersonal relationships. They may grow up anxious and suspicious, afraid of being hurt if they become too close to another person. They fear making the same mistake their parents made and have difficulty letting themselves become dependent on anyone. As adults they are more likely to divorce than those who grow up in intact families. Some, on the other hand, become far more conservative than their parents.

CIVILIZED DIVORCE

Luckily, not all children of divorce suffer the problems described in the preceding section. Even so grandparents have a significant role.

Lucile and Her Mother

Lucile, an attractive, single, authoritative mother with 7 and 10-year-old girls, told us about her divorce. "My husband and I finally decided to go our separate ways after years of drifting apart. We sat down with the children and explained that we would get a divorce and not live together but that the children would still have both of us. We are good friends and take care not to badmouth each other. He sees them twice a month and takes them a month each summer. I am a strict disciplinarian and insist that my children mind. We live with my folks and they use the same technique. As grandparents I think they are easier on their grandchildren than they were on me when I was that age. But they are wonderful, and I am very thankful that they are around to take care of my children while I work."

We asked Lucile's mother about the divorce. She said, "We had been expecting it for some time. In the interval between the first and second child, there was a growing sense of frustration over their new role as parents which culminated in a divorce when the children were one and five years old. It was sad. Our five-year-old granddaughter, Melissa, experienced the usual anxieties. She was sad, felt guilty, and was afraid she would be abandoned. She kept trying to reunite the family.

"I am angry at John, my ex son-in-law. He never grew up. He was a devoted father but a completely irresponsible husband. But to his credit he continues to see the children. I am sorry for Lucile. She supports herself and the children with very little help. She works full time as a nurse, 12 hour shifts, to reduce the number of days away from them.

"Of course we enjoy having them here. Children need grandparents, especially in single parent families. They need to know what the family considers important. Moral and spiritual values can be shared. We are there to listen and advise. We try to let them know that we will always be around to help them grow up."

LOSS OF SELF ESTEEM

Other children of divorce are less fortunate. When a parent leaves, the child is also usually "divorced." If Dad leaves, many children not illogically reason that it means the child is not worth enough for Dad to stay, that the child does not deserve the parent's care and love. Baumrind's study showed that divorcing fathers were (on the average) more abrasive toward their children both before and after the divorce. This problem compounds itself over time because over half of all fathers do not pay the court ordered child support. When they do pay, it usually is too little to allow the child the same standard of living as before. One result — single mothers and their children form the largest group of America's poor.

When the child reaches eighteen most fathers cut off payment and do not help with college even though fathers usually increase their own standard of living after divorce. Thus children of divorce rarely achieve the same degree of education as their fathers. This further reduces the young adult's self-esteem and interferes with the full development of his potential. These descriptions fortunately do not fit every father in divorce.

THE SINGLE PERMISSIVE PARENT

Divorce frequently leads to permissive child rearing. Most single mothers have to work and by their very absence permit the child to do many things he wouldn't be allowed to do if mother was home. After work mother faces another full time job in keeping up the home. Often she feels guilty for being gone or simply lacks the energy to really demand good behavior and follow through with discipline, or even to respond fully to the child's needs. Permissively raised children don't become very competent. They don't do as well in school. More often than not children of single parents come home to an empty house. Latch key children get into trouble with drugs twice as much as children with mothers at home. All of these uncomfortable facts demonstrate the vital need for grandparents to enter the picture.

DIVORCE AND ADOLESCENTS

Divorce can exacerbate normal adolescent rebellion. Adolescents especially need family structure, stability and values. Establishing structure, which involves setting standards and limits, is more effective when both parents participate. This helps the control of normal teenage impulsiveness, of their inner turmoil and anxieties. Structure gives teenagers a base of security and the confidence which enables them to develop into normal, competent and socially responsible adults. It reduces drug abuse and premature sexual activity. Divorce can also represent a personal rejection to adolescents. They feel humiliated, hurt and angry. During the teen years many cope with their feelings by running away and taking their chances on the street. Others cope in different ways.

Tina

Dr. Judith Wallerstein followed what happened to Tina for the fifteen years of her research study reported in her book, *Second Chances*:

"The first time I met Tina — a tall willowy sixteen-year-old with brown hair and striking blue eyes — she had just had a fight with her mother on the way to my office. 'She almost wouldn't drive me here,' she said, wiping away a tear. 'Now it's her back that hurts, but I told her what I think — what a great trick she's pulling on us. She's not sick and I told her to get out of bed.'

"'Are you all right, Tina?'

"'Thank you, I'm fine,' she said, running fingers through her pixie haircut. 'I just get so emotional. I guess I could have used help a long time ago, but now I don't need it that much because I've talked a lot of this out with my grandparents and my brothers. Now I want to forget it.' Tina was laughing and crying at the same time.

"'It's not so easy to forget things that hurt you, I said.

"'I'm too emotional,' Tina said, 'just like my dad. He's a lawyer, you know.' I had already heard a great deal about Tina's father from her mother and the other children in the family, all of whom had told me that he yelled at everyone around him.

"'My dad and I are alike,' Tina went on. 'I can talk to him. Sure, he's not perfect and he says terrible things to Mom — that she's a parasite, a taker — but the truth is, there are probably a lot of weaknesses on both sides. Sometimes I feel like I'm the parent. My folks should be more mature.'

"When I asked about her mother, Tina surprised me with her insight when she said, 'I worry that Mom is never going to get her act together, even though she's always been there for us kids, has always tried her best. She's always going to be looking for something she can't find. She's got more hangups than you could name. I really worry about her, and I still feel responsible. She's really been down on herself lately. I don't want to make it worse and I don't want her to know how I worry about her. I guess the thing I resent most about their divorce is not knowing the truth. Mom says one thing and Dad says another, and it's unreal, just like a damn soap opera with Dad on one end of the couch and Mom on the other.'

"When I saw Tina a few weeks later, we talked about her plans for her future. 'I will not be like my mother.' she said emphatically. 'I want to have a career and do well at school, and maybe I'll be a lawyer, or maybe I'll marry a lawyer, or maybe I'll be a legal aide. Maybe I'll go onstage, but I'm not going to marry young.' In the meantime, Tina had decided to live with her mother. 'Dad is unbearable,' she said, holding her arms out as if balancing a weight in each hand. 'Mom needs me.' Indeed, Tina listened sympathetically to her mother's complaints, assuring her that she would never be abandoned."

GRANDPARENT'S INVOLVEMENT

Children of divorce suffer more than many were willing to believe. They badly need help and next to their parents the most logical source is their grandparents. But some grandparents offer many reasons to avoid becoming involved with grandchildren, with or without divorce, especially if the children are difficult to deal with. Some few reject the grandparenting role anyway because of the implication that it is associated with old age — and they don't want to appear old. Some feel too tired. Or they may feel that they have no authority and don't want to butt in. Often, grandparents who try to avoid active grandparenting have no memory of exposure to their own grandparents. Rootless themselves, without a model, they have trouble feeling comfortable in the role.

Many grandparents feel that they did a poor job of parenting their now adult children. In some cases their children grew up into problem adults. The instinctive guilt feelings which go with normal parenting have already been aggravated by the litany of critics who blame almost every person's problems on their parents. This increases the sense of guilt and the hurt it brings with it. Such feelings seem worse when the parent is around an adult child who represents a parental failure. It can be even worse when the adult child objects to the way grandparents try to discipline or control the grandchild. It is easy to infringe on the parent's territory, even without meaning to.

The combination of all these factors makes it easier to withdraw than to be involved with the grandchildren.

A good number of grandparents withdraw completely. But in spite of their negative attitudes and tough talk, most of them still help when their children and grandchildren have troubles. When divorce occurs, their actions don't follow their professed and somewhat hostile sounding philosophy. Colleen Johnson, an anthropologist digging in contemporary San Francisco, found that involved grandmothers defined their role as an advocate for the grandchild, even to the point of mediating with the parents. They recognized the need to be there, to love and provide security, stability, family and continuity. Most of the "San Francisco group" of grandparents she studied gave financial and supportive help. Around a third became active parents again in spite of their reservations about such involvement.

PARENTS TAKING SIDES

Dr. Judith Wallerstein, after long and careful study of divorce emphasizes that grandparents should stay out of their adult children's divorce struggles. The problems may increase if grandparents take sides. This can institutionalize and traditionalize the fight, increasing and prolonging the ill feelings, thus aggravating the effects on the grandchildren. However if withdrawal from the squabbling family is too complete it could make it difficult to help the grandchildren. Still, staying out of the fight usually makes it easier to support the grandchildren. Such support becomes especially important when the parents are so bound up in their own problems that they either ignore the children or, worse, try to recruit them on their side of the dispute.

One exception to the "stay out of the mess" advice occurs when trouble starts brewing in a marriage from obvious mental problems on the part of your own married adult-child. Many of these appear to be inherited disorders of brain chemistry. They may have less to do with how children were raised than used to be thought. Depression, schizophrenia and alcoholism often do not appear until the late teens or early adult life. Frequently a family history of such disorders exists. This can be used as a way of approaching the subject, to call attention to the problem and the similarities of the symptoms. It also helps when you can offer examples of family members who overcame their problems with help. Medication, psychiatric care, Alcoholics Anonymous and other sources of care exist. Encouraging early treatment may avoid potential divorce and produce a better family for your grandchildren to grow in.

Adult children considering divorce frequently go to their parents for advice. However, offering advice can be particularly challenging and requires almost professional diplomacy — like most grandparents have learned to use, including Janice's Dad.

Janice's Dad

Janice's dad helped her by being a good listener when she turned to him for advice as she considered divorcing her excessively jealous and domineering husband. She was receiving marriage counseling from her pastor who advised staying married above all. However, her husband would not let her handle money or have a checking account. He refused to let her drive or have a car and became violent and abusive when she made contact with anyone besides him, even with her parents. In counseling he was so adamant about his possessiveness that the pastor became alarmed. Janice's father was somewhat aware of the problems. When she called he let her tell her story. He offered questions to help her crystalize her feelings and guided her to her own solution without any direct advice except, "Honey, if you divorce him, don't run away. Walk away." He offered to take her three-year-old for awhile if it would help.

WAYS GRANDPARENTS HELP

One of the biggest problems of divorce is that the mother usually is left with the child and a greatly diminished income. To help the mother and grandchild requires real sensitivity to their feelings. Recognizing the blow to the ego of adult-children forced to depend again on Mom and Dad, grandparents often find ways of making their help look less threatening. They pay for more items when shopping with their children, or give large birthday, Christmas and Hanukkah gifts. Many help with funds for the education of grandchildren or with the purchase of a house. Do it as a partnership to avoid the feeling of the adult-child that she has lost the equality with her parents which she had achieved when she grew up and became an adult. This ego problem may be the root of a mother's resentment of advice from her parents about child rearing. Regardless, grandparents can support the parent and child in many ways. One key is being available to the grandchildren.

Spending time with the child imparts a sense of family strength and continuity. Grandparents who live nearby may be able to help by picking the child up after school and keeping him while mother works, thus avoiding the loneliness and vulnerability of a latch key existence. Of course Mother is lonely too. Divorce changes the network of friends for both Mother and Father. Many of their previously close friends may become distant after divorce. This offers another reason for grandparents to help fill the vacuum. Many grandparents find themselves representing the family and child at parent-teacher conferences when neither parent can attend.

"Babysitting" the child some evenings so mother can get other necessary things done, including social functions, also helps. In this day and age of quick travel the child can fly down to spend a weekend with his grandparents. If they live too far away at least routine telephone calls to the child can be made, post cards or letters can be sent. The routine itself becomes very important because the child may have little other stability in life. Express interest in his school work, play and other normal events in the life of the child. Most importantly grandparents can listen to and be interested in what the child feels and says, remaining neutral about the parents in the divorce struggle. Avoid emphasizing the separation. Emphasis should be more on both parents' good qualities rather than the bad. It also helps to let the child know that his parents loved each other when they decided to have him, even if they don't love each other now.

The Divorced Daughter-In-Law

It is not always advisable for grandparents to avoid the ex-daughter-in-law or son-in-law. Stay as neutral as possible. Emphasize the positive and admirable aspects of both parents. Done diplomatically this helps reduce friction. More importantly it allows the grandparents greater access to the grandchildren. Sometimes the paternal grandmother forms a friendship with her ex-daughter-in-law. This allows more interaction and support of the grandchildren and aids the single working mother whose needs for financial support and help with the children may be overwhelming. The example of Susan and how she handled the problem of keeping in touch with her grandchildren offers valuable lessons.

Susan and Laura

Susan, a grandmotherly retired nurse, was stunned when her daughter-in-law tearfully called and said, "John's left. He, he wants a divorce. He said he can't stand me anymore!" Susan had noticed that her son had seemed preoccupied when they had attended a family wedding together a few months before. But John and Laura had seemed to be getting along, and the grandchildren had seemed happy. Jennie, age three and Mike age six were the apple of Susan's eye. It just didn't seem possible. With a sinking feeling in her stomach she realized that Laura would most likely take the children. And while Laura had always been civil to her mother-in-law she had never been close or really warmed up to her. Susan told Laura that she would fly down from her home in New Hampshire to help with the grandchildren, and Laura agreed.

Susan bought her tickets to Connecticut that next morning. But she had just gotten home from the travel agency when Laura called again, almost hysterical and angry, "I've decided that I don't want you to come," she said in a strained voice and then rambled on about John and the other woman he had moved in with.

Susan listened and didn't comment until Laura had finished her complaints. Then she gently said, "Laura, I already have the tickets and the reservations. I'll rent a car at the airport and will be over to see Jenny and Mike by early afternoon. It will be good to see you again too, dear. You don't really mind do you?"

Laura hesitated and then said "Ok," in a low voice. When Susan hung up she hurt deeply inside for Laura, and worried about what this would do to Jenny and Mike. She knew that Laura wasn't close to her but she relied on past experience when Laura had seemed pleased that the children enjoyed "grandmaw" when she was around. She kept repeating this to herself as she drove to Laura's from the airport. John hadn't called and she didn't have his new phone number or address.

When she arrived at the front door she smiled and said, "Hello dear!" to Laura, gave her a hug, and went immediately to the grand-children. Jennie and Mike swarmed over her while they exchanged hugs and kisses and important information about Mike's new trans-former and Jenny's new doll. Later Susan neutrally heard Laura out and got John's new address and telephone number. She told Laura that her real interest in coming was to check on Jenny and Mike and see if she could help them.

Susan complimented Laura on what a good job she was doing with the children and said, "I am so pleased that you are keeping the children out of this. It's really important that we all try our best to protect them from being involved. Children need to think well of both their mother and father so I am not going to say anything bad about anybody! I can stay for the rest of the week so if you want I will be happy to watch the kids while you do what you have to do. And Easter vacation will be coming up soon. You and the children, or even just them, could come up to visit for the week. I would love it!"

John remarried and he and his new wife have the children two days a week. Susan keeps in touch with all of them, carefully avoiding any body language or overt expressions of impatience with the parents or stepparents. She talks with the grandchildren about "safe" subjects and her interest in the family is obviously centered around the grandchildren. Although they live a distance apart she manages to spend several weeks a year with them. Every holiday, birthday or request from either Laura or John results in grandmother happily "baby sitting." Over time Laura became less reserved with her ex-mother-in-law, went to school part time with some help from Susan, and became a financially secure certified public accountant.

EXCLUDED

Sometimes the bitter feelings in divorce spill over onto the grandparents. As a result some mothers and fathers refuse to let their ex-in-laws, the child's grandparents on the "other side", see their children. Some grandparents have gone to court to get legal visiting rights. Fifty states passed laws giving grandparents the right to petition the courts for legally enforced visiting rights. This raises the issue of what is best for the child. Does the good influence of the grandparents always outweigh the family conflict created or aggravated by the court proceedings? The conflict can put the child in the middle and in the position of having to choose sides. Some psychologists and lawyers feel that the child is not always well served by the proceedings. On the other hand the fact that such laws exist may make it easier in some cases to approach a reluctant parent and negotiate for visiting privileges.

Certainly children need grandparents, but their need for their parents generally takes priority. If grandparents recognize this and approach the issue diplomatically, respecting parental rights, court fights can often be avoided. Most importantly, keep the grandchildren out of the negotiations, out of any conflict. Recognition that the children may be hurt by the strife, and clearly watching out for their best interests, allows grandparents a better chance to develop a positive relationship with the parent and the grandchildren. Going in aggressively increases tensions. Don't approach the problem with a chip on your shoulder. Start slowly with presents, birthday cards, low key letters and telephone calls about positive family events etc. Try to do something nice and say something nice about the parent who has custody of the grandchildren. Concentrate on the good things they are doing or have done. Don't rush the effort, go a step at a time. Concentrate on what you have to give the grandchild in the way of the security of roots, support and stimulation, without strings. Try to avoid putting a guilt trip on the reluctant parent because guilt generally creates more resentment. It is not wise to take sides in the divorce struggle. Usually it is not wise to even express an opinion about your feelings on the divorce or the troubles between your son and his ex-wife. Instead, state your ground rules, that your interest is in the grandchildren, period.

Some parents are truly dysfunctional and bad for their children. If you think that is the case, first read the next chapter which concentrates on dysfunctional parents and grandparents. You may find it helpful to talk the problems over with a professional counselor before you act. That approach is a lot less expensive than the courts. Sometimes you may be unaware of how you come across to the parents of your grandchildren. They want respect and if they believe that you don't respect them, or that you have taken sides in the divorce struggle, then they will often try to keep the children away. A change in your approach may help. It is important that society has begun to recognize that grandchildren have the right to have access to their grandparents. The bottom line is that grandparents can have a positive effect on the child. If the parent is really dysfunctional and doing the child harm, and you can help, then the courts are there to use.

GRANDPARENTING THE CHILDREN

When Susan has the grandchildren she gives them more freedom to play than she did with her own children. But limits still exist and she simply has to show her authority by telling them, "All right, Grandma means business!" Their love and respect for her make control easy.

Some grandparents might worry that they are being taken advantage of. More and more grandparents find themselves parenting their grandchildren directly, often almost full time. Some, when forced by circumstances to parent grandchildren, try to avoid disciplining. Most grandparents want their time with the grandchildren to be fun and often feel they can't discipline *and* have fun. But it is never too late to learn — even for grandparents who raised their own children permissively.

In Chapter Two, we discussed studies which show that permissively raised children don't turn out as well as children of rational-authoritative or traditional parents. Even if you raised your children permissively, the need for change in attitude and techniques in raising your grandchildren can overshadow your innate resistance to change. You *can* teach an old dog new tricks! Most grandparents are young enough, flexible enough and bright enough to improve their own parenting techniques when they find themselves, like it or not, parenting their own grandchildren.

Sensible (rational-authoritative) grandparenting makes the job more fun. Wisely using grandparental powers enables control of children with less anger and hostility. The fun involved in loving and nurturing children continues. Added to this reward come many satisfactions. First, you can take pride in the way your grandchildren respond to sensible grandparenting. You can also take pride when you find yourself used as an admired model, both by the parents of your grandchildren and the grandchildren themselves.

Sensible grandparenting methods makes grandchildren happier and more secure. It encourages the development of their competence. They also tend to adopt the values you really live by. Even if you don't like the idea of taking care of your grandchild, the fact that you do anyway represents an important basic value that they recognize. In turn they begin to reflect the sense of responsibility they see in their grandparents. Faith in a grandparent's consistent nurturing builds the child's sense of personal responsibility. They do mimic us.

THE REWARDS FOR GRANDPARENTS

Children admire and emulate their grandparents. This became apparent during a follow-up interview with Dr. Wallerstein.

"Now, at our ten-year interview, Tina at twenty-six has grown into a lovely, lively young woman whose warm smile and open manner make her a pleasure to be with. Her hair is still cut short, and she wears large horn-rimmed glasses that make her look scholarly. Although we are sitting in a crowded cafeteria, she has no compunction about telling me deeply personal facts about her life. She has just started to practice law at a prestigious firm, and I can imagine her in a courtroom — brash, competent, intelligent, and fast on the verbal draw.

"I ask about her family. 'Mom is okay,' she says with a hint of a sigh. 'She's still looking for something she can't find. I've gotten used to it. I used to feel guilty and thought I should stay with her and help her out all the time. I still worry about her, but I'm not as frightened as I used to be. She's not working or anything.' Tina taps her fingers on the Formica tabletop for a moment, as if to nudge her memory. 'I remember Mom getting more and more depressed and not being able to cope. I tried to stay home all I could. Gee, I remember at home we used to hide under the covers and shake when they were fighting.'

"And her father? 'I admire him. He's bright and he has a sense of humor, but he's a real Dr. Jekyll and Mr. Hyde. When he's bad, he's terrible. On the other hand, I find his approval very important. But I can't work in the same city with him. My law firm is in Sacramento and his is in San Francisco. That's well and good.' Tina reflects more carefully for a moment and adds, 'I'm glad that my drive to achieve comes from my dad, but he could have been a lot nicer to Mom. Most people have at least a semblance of civility. If it weren't for my grandparents, I don't think I could have made it past sixteen.'

"Tina warms to the subject of her grandparents. 'When my mom and dad were acting like babies, my grandparents became my parents. They still are. Going home for me is going to their house in Sonoma. I worry about them a lot. Grandma is seventy-six and Grandpa is seventy-nine. It's hard to see them getting older, but watching them together is wonderful. One couldn't survive without the other. It's been important for me to see that. I still look to them in times of crisis. They've been a rock for all of us kids. I couldn't have made it through college without their help, financial and emotional.'"

We asked Tina's grandparents how they had handled the divorce — and Tina during the divorce. Did they talk with Tina about her parents? "No," replied Grandfather, "we were uncomfortable talking with her about her parents. When the subject came up we remained neutral and steered the conversation to other things. Mostly we listened to her and talked about her dreams, ambitions and her social life. We did help her financially get through law school." Grand- mother chimed in, "We are always so pleased to have Tina visit. She has stayed in our spare bedroom, I don't know how many times. If she is busy we always called her every week. Still do!" she said with a smile.

Many grandmothers don't believe they can ever become per- fect grandparents. They find it difficult to keep their emotions under control and are still angry at one or both of their grandchild's parents. Some doubt that they can learn the sensible, rational and authoritative parenting methods recommended here. Actually, it isn't that hard. All you have to do is walk on water! But even if we don't become perfect, we still have a very positive effect. For example, Helen's maternal grandmother had taken Helen and her mother in after Helen's mother and father had divorced. It wasn't a very comfortable situation and Helen had little good to say about her grandmother. She described her as, "A harpy, prickly, cold and critical person." Yet Helen said that when her grandmother died, "I cried and cried. My grandmother, even as one of the worst grandmothers, had a very positive influence in my life and had been supportive through difficult times."

Probably Mankind has not yet been perfected —

there is room for further evolution. —Robert A. Aldrich, M.D.

8 TROUBLED FAMILIES

Parents and perfection rarely go hand in hand. So children put up with a certain amount of imperfection. Most are loved enough that they thrive, and when they grow up they often become somewhat better parents than their parents were. However not all children thrive. A limit exists on their ability to adapt to adversity. And some parents and some grandparents are worse than not perfect. A few can only be described as plain bad. But good or bad. they had children.

To be around their grandchildren some grandparents have to deal with bad parents and troubled families. The troubles we discuss in this chapter are severe: alcoholism, drug abuse, child abuse and molestation, mental illness and uncontrolled temper. Families with such troubles function poorly — the current buzz word for them is 'dysfunctional.' The dysfunction can arise from many sources, including the family roots. Sometimes it is genetic in origin and sometimes psychological; in either case it is often passed on to the children and possibly even to the grandchildren. It may originate with any of the grandchild's four grandparents or be passed on through genes they carried even if they weren't afflicted with the problem themselves.

Some grandparents were and some still are dysfunctional. Some of us were not at all ready for the responsibility of parenting when we had our own children. We may have been too preoccupied with our own serious personal problems, or perhaps our own parents were not good role models so we didn't know how to parent well. Poor parenting often creates a new generation of dysfunctional families. So, if you were handicapped as a parent and didn't do a very good job, you may have had a role in creating the dysfunctional family your grandchild is being raised in. In that case, both you and your adult-child need to learn better parenting methods. Luckily, you now have the grandparent's advantage of more maturity even if you were dysfunctional in the past. You probably find that you are a more sensible grandparent than you were a parent. Now, by being the best grandparent you can be, you can make a significant difference in the outcome of your grandchild's troubled family.

Even if you were not one of the root causes of the troubles and were not and are not dysfunctional, if you have to deal with a dysfunctional family you will need all the information about such families you can find. Both the definitions and the estimates of the numbers of dysfunctional families vary widely. Some adult-children blame *all* of their problems on their parents whom they feel were dysfunctional, and a few seem to feel that most parents are dysfunctional and incapable. Here we concentrate on those severely troubled families who may put your grandchildren at risk.

Certainly a lot of parents functioned poorly in the past — and do now. Many adults today bear emotional and even physical scars left over from childhood. On the other hand, less than a hundred years ago it was considered great if the children survived, much less had a comfortable life or turned out perfectly.

Parents and History

History offers us a less negative perspective about today's troubled parents. Overall, the well-being of humanity has increased over the centuries. But expectations exceed reality in modern American society. Periods of bare survival, regression or tyranny spurred parents of the past to create a better life for themselves and their children. It is hard to imagine how we would react to the conditions of the past that shaped our ancestors. Epidemics of plague and small-pox repeatedly killed close to half of the population of Europe. Harsh tyrannical rule by emperors, kings, landowners and bosses was the expected norm. Some of these pressures were passed on by parents to their children. Famine and war kept the population down. Children were needed to help farm. Men outlived their wives who died by the millions in childbirth, or from the labor of trying to keep a home intact without modern appliances. The survival of children was often brief.

The human race is remarkably resilient. Children not only survived dysfunctional parents, they survived dysfunctional societies. Evolution advanced us from the cave men, through the brutality of ancient civilized Rome and the London slums of Victorian times where one out of every four infants diet of malnourishment. Charles Dickens in eighteenth century England wrote movingly of the horrible conditions children grew up in. Children were thought of and treated as small and therefore unimportant adults. The majority of the population of London was reputed at one time to usually be drunk on gin. Yet the progeny of Oliver Twist's times survived and improved their conditions and that of their children. In the United States in the not too distant past some six and seven-year-olds worked in factories and coal mines up to twelve hours a day. In our day we witnessed the terrible dysfunction of Nazi Germany and Stalinist Russia. Their people are throwing off the yoke of dictatorship and taking control of their future. Grandparents, individually, can throw off the yoke of their own dysfunction and take control of themselves.

The advances of the last centuries, crafted by the reformation and the industrial revolution, have been phenomenal. The changes in our lifetime continue at a breathtaking rate. Revolutions — political, economical, technical, and moral — have become the order of the day. Social structures have been shattered, rebuilt, and shattered again. The uncertainties and anxieties created by the lack of social stability and structure are enough to drive a person to drink or drugs; many have been so driven. Yet the overall effect of the changes, the overall results have been positive. Certainly we have been wasteful of resources, careless about the environment, and have taken many paths up blind alleys away from the road of positive evolution. That has to change. And yes, the population explosion creates a crisis which must be faced.

In spite of all these problems we are more affluent, live longer and healthier lives, are better educated and informed and have more opportunities in life than all our ancestors before us. The bottom line is that in spite of all these problems our ancestors did remarkably well by us. We, our parents, children and grandchildren have cause for pride and much to celebrate. But we still must ask ourselves if *we* are as good ancestors as our forefathers were when we consider the sophisticated and ample resources existing today? Well, although many of us created problems for our children, we still accomplished a lot and gave our children a lot in spite of our imperfections.

THE HALF FULL GLASS

Many of us have been unable to shake off the results of our personal history, of our parents' imperfections. The confusion accompanying the dizzying and sometimes wrenching changes in our society often makes it harder to improve. Yet as grandparents and parents we still have a lot to offer. We become even more important in this period of mass merchandising, mass production, mass education and mass transportation. Grandparents each offer something that current society cannot — personal roots, personal attention and the personal caring which confirms individuality. We may be flawed, but we are still the best and sometimes the only adult personally and meaningfully available to our grandchildren. We are family. We grandparents are survivors!

THE HALF EMPTY GLASS

Some individuals, as has occurred throughout history, become completely lost in the changes of society. For whatever reason, they have sunk into drug abuse, alcoholism, immorality or crime. Each of these individuals is someone's child and each of their children is someone's grandchild. These children may be abused and neglected, and that should not be allowed. They are too vulnerable, valuable and precious to allow them to be harmed. Still, many survive and turn out well in spite of incompetent parents. They are tough.

We can take only limited comfort in the viability, toughness and adaptability of our grandchildren. Although children in alcoholic families learn to adapt, they often grow up with a distorted view of life. Children who suffer emotional or physical abuse may have low self-esteem. When they become parents they tend to repeat that abuse on their children. More often than not we tend to mirror our own parent's behavior, even if we didn't like it. Look at the experience of Louella:

Louella

"My grandmother had not wanted my mother to marry my father and she was always pointing out his faults. Most of her remarks were absolutely true. He went out with other women, he was out drinking three or four nights a week until two or three AM. My grandmother criticized my father in front of me. My mother would always defend my father. As I got older I realized that she was also an alcoholic. I remember her screaming at me and slapping me. At times like that my grandmother would pack up and leave.

"When I became a parent I remembered how my parents abused me and vowed not to be a parent like they were. I knew what I didn't want to do but didn't know what to do. As a result I didn't control my child and he began to abuse me. I was so angry I felt like screaming at him and slapping him.

"In spite of the fact that grandmother left when things got out of hand with my parents fighting or hitting me, I realize now that she did all she could. She was a source of stability and caring. Even her leaving taught me a lesson. Don't put up with abuse! Her leaving gave my parents a message that they were impossible. Her example gave me the courage to leave later."

The Mirror

One of the best things we can do as grandparents is to look at ourselves. After all, where did these dysfunctional parents come from? From us or from that other set of grandparents? And how did we or they get that way? Most likely by the way we were raised by our parents. The important thing is not to concentrate on blame. Instead each of us can try to parent our adult-children and our grandchildren a little better than we were parented. The message we receive from Louella is that we need to learn to improve our parenting. The message isn't that we should blame our parents or grandparents. Blaming them is a cop-out because it offers a way to absolve us of our personal responsibility for our actions. It may be comforting to blame but it is hardly productive.

As grandparents we each have two questions to ask ourselves, "Was I dysfunctional or not as a parent? How can I become more functional now that I am a grandparent?" Second, "Regardless of whether I was an admirable or poor parent, how do I help my grand-child if he happens to have dysfunctional parents?" Let's start with those of us who were incontestably terrible parents and are probably not much better as grandparents.

Problem Grandparents: The Almost Empty Glass

Some of today's grandparents did a terrible job of parenting. They had uncontrollable tempers and physically abused their children, often during alcoholic binges. They may have disliked one of their children because he was "just like his father," and treated him poorly as a result. They may have spent too little time caring for their children or were excessively critical and angry at their children. In more seriously troubled families, a parent may have physically or sexually abused his children or abused drugs and abandoned the child. The laundry list of problems we don't like to talk about can be long and bothersome.

If you as a grandparent still cannot control your alcoholism, immature sexual urges, temper or hypercritical attitude it may be best to keep your distance during troubled times. By this exercise in self control you demonstrate your basic values of love and responsibility. Do no harm. Stay away.

If small children make you nervous, irritable and critical, don't visit often or for long stretches of time. Call them instead, send postcards and letters. Remember birthdays and holidays. Remembrance, even from black-sheep parents and grandparents, has great value. It says that you still love and care, and it validates the importance of your children and grandchildren. It's never too late to show love.

At the same time, many grandparents with problems eventually overcome them and are then able to contribute to the lives of their grandchildren. They become shining models of the ability to overcome adversity and one's own problems. This ability to "reform" creates double joy. First comes the pride of learning self-control at any age. Second comes the satisfaction of being able to help and enjoy both the children and the grandchildren. You may find that living with and surviving your problems gives you some surprising strengths which enable you to contribute productively to your family's lives.

STRENGTHS OF GRANDPARENTS WHOSE FAMILIES FUNCTIONED POORLY

1. Learning from the problems they experienced in the past, grandparents are often motivated to be less impulsive and will take the time to make sensible, careful judgments.

2. Over time, grandparents have usually learned that fighting within the family often leads to unwise decisions, so they now know how to wait until a rational solution is possible before forcing a confrontation.

3. The inflexibility that grandparents may have had as parents usually softens with time and now can become a source of reliability to grandchildren.

4. Grandparents who have formerly been very fearful of harsh judgments and criticisms can now empathize with their adult-children's reactions to criticism and become more accepting and supporting of both their children and grandchildren.

5. Grandparents who now understand that they were over-critical in the past learn to use a new and more friendly attitude with both their adult-children and the grandchildren.

6. Remembering their own great need for approval helps grandparents understand the grandchild's need for recognition and approval.

7. Questioning their past parenting skills allows grandparents to be receptive to learning better methods and attitudes. The can learn how to listen calmly, respect the feelings of others, cooperate and then develop reasoned responses after adequate thought.

8. Most grandparents who were rejecting, neglecting, too authoritarian or too permissive in the past have learned enough from their past experience to become more sensible in their own grandparenting.

9. Recognizing that they could have done a better job in raising their children and being wise enough to know that they need help, mature grandparents often take child-rearing courses or seek individual counseling to improve their techniques and attitudes. This allows better relations with both their now adult-children and their grandchildren.

In other words, practice improves anyone's performance and grandparents, by virtue of the fact that they have parented before, bring valuable experience to the job. This is particularly true when grandparents can be open-minded and objective about their past parenting performance. Your improvement can make a big difference in how effective you are in meeting your grandchild's needs, especially if his parents are dysfunctional.

WHEN YOUR ADULT-CHILD IS DYSFUNCTIONAL

In earlier chapters we discussed some of the ways that those of us who were poor parents can become productive grandparents. However, it is harder to change someone else than it is to change ourselves, especially when that someone else is your adult-child or his or her spouse.

Fortunately, as grandparents we have more going for us than when we were young. Most of us learned that rewards are more effective than criticisms. We know enough to stay out of our adult-child's marital squabbles and have learned to refrain from criticizing the way they raise their children. We have also seen ways by which parents can encourage troubled adult-children to seek help by talking about the success stories of others. But often we are still bothered by the question of why our adult-child married a dysfunctional spouse? Understanding why may give us clues which can help us improve our relations with both our dysfunctional adult-child, the spouse and the grandchildren.

Why Did She Marry Joe?

One of the first questions many of us ask when a son or daughter marries an irresponsible or violent spouse, is why did he or she marry such a person? Probably few of our children would have married a spouse like that if they had known what that person was really like prior to the marriage. It might be reasonable before marriage to tell the kids to hold off until they get to know the parents and family of their sweetheart. People often reflect many characteristics of their family-of-origin. This might cool off some budding romances. The spouse-to-be will probably end up parenting the way he or she was parented, or do the complete opposite. This will have a major effect on your grandchildren, but you will have a hard time convincing your child of this. It may be better not to try. Not only is young love blind and deaf to advice, the spouse-to-be usually looks like perfection incarnate to your child because the heat waves from love distort perceptions.

However, once the hormonal and emotional rushes leading to marriage have subsided, things often change. Typically, the hearts and flowers before marriage obscured each partner's deepest needs. Sometimes they were not even aware of these needs before. Subconsciously, one may look for a dominant husband who seems just right because he is harsh and authoritarian just like Dad. Another may look for a wife to bully, a slave to answer every whim as perhaps his own mother did. The personality types and desires are as numerous and different as people, and little thought is given to what the loved one will be like after marriage.

Before being too harsh on your adult-child for having made a bad choice, recognize that things might have developed after marriage that could not have been anticipated. Teenagers who appear to be normal can become mentally ill as young adults. For example, manic-depression rarely manifests itself until the late teen years or beyond. Alcoholism can be triggered by psychological problems created by job or emotional stresses. Normal feeling and acting individuals may find themselves having violent temper tantrums aimed at the spouse they considered perfect during courtship. They find their inner-child-of-the-past suddenly taking over and the result might be wife-beating or child abuse. Other immaturities can suddenly appear: sexual abuse, infidelity, lying and cheating — tendencies which were buried before under the powerful force of romantic love. Benjamin Franklin wrote in one of his "letters to a nephew" that the age of reason for a young man is 26! It takes at least a hundred years to fully civilize a person and that veneer, which we hope will control any personality problems, may turn out to be rather thin. Unpleasant surprises can result.

One of the remarkable phenomena in marriage is the ability, almost the compulsion, to put up with a dysfunctional spouse. The wives of wife-beaters forgive and crawl back. The husband's of witches retreat to their Casper Milk Toast corner. The spouse of an alcoholic will defend and aid. Even wives of men who sexually molest their own children will clamp on a lid of secrecy. If problems of this sort occur, the first thing grandparents should do is increase their knowledge about the problems and the solutions.

GETTING HELP

One excellent source of information is the book, *Women Who Love Too Much* by Robin Norwood. It offers penetrating explanations about why women put up with various forms of abuse and neglect and some pathways to healing are suggested. Carol Travis's book, *Anger, The Misunderstood Emotion*, offers a sobering look at the results of anger and some practical suggestions on control. One of the clearest and most perceptive books written on personality development is Hugh Misseldine's book, *Your Inner Child of the Past*. Claudette Wassill-Grimm's book, *How To Avoid Your Parents' Mistakes When Raising Your Children*, gives the reader a close and personal look at how adult-children of dysfunctional parents learn to parent effectively. Glenn Austin's *Love and Power/Parent and Child*, offers grandparents and parents ways to improve parenting effectiveness. In addition many public schools, community hospitals, YMCAs and community colleges offer valuable parenting courses which can increase your understanding of the attitudes and emotions of your grandchildren's parents.

Your dysfunctional adult-children will probably resent it if you try to counsel them directly. Even more when the advice is true — guilt feelings are often protected by lashing out at anyone who brings up the problem. Even if they directly ask you for advice, be cautious. Let them do most of the talking and try to subtly guide the conversation so *they* verbalize the need for help. Then, if you happen to know of a good therapist whom you can recommend, suggest that they seek professional help. Be lighthanded, even lighthearted and positive. Perhaps suggesting that they talk the problem over with the family doctor or the children's pediatrician might be less threatening. If you have the funds, an offer of financial help may speed things along. The best strategy might be to have a family member or friend who has suffered the same problem get together with the dysfunctional individual and offer understanding and help.

John

The police had been called by a neighbor who heard Stacy screaming. John had blackened her eye and bruised her badly when he broke a chair over her back as she tried to run out of the apartment. Stacy had refused to sign a complaint but the police told John that if he beat her again they would take him to jail, complaint or no complaint. John's mother had been aware of his temper, but was shocked when she saw Stacy and also recognized that their child, Darla, had witnessed the attack. Her deceased husband had a violent temper as had his brothers. Stirred into action by the sight of Stacy's bruises and the scared look on four-year-old Darla's face, grandmother decided to intervene.

One of her husband's brothers had conquered his violent temper by going to group counseling. So Grandmother invited him to dinner along with John, Stacy and Darla. He looked at Stacy's receding bruises, and, when the story came out, suggested that John see his counselor. "Those sessions were fascinating, John," he said, "and I learned a lot about me. Too bad your father couldn't have taken the same treatment. I learned more about myself than I had ever suspected. And I have felt better about myself since. All of my brothers and I remembered our Dad beating Mom. It's bad for kids to grow up watching that sort of stuff. I'll bet it scared Darla when you hurt Stacy, didn't it?"

WHEN HELP DOESN'T HELP:
THE REALLY BAD PROBLEMS

What if the couple resists help? They still parent your grandchildren. Some grandparents find that ignoring the parents' behavior and treating them warmly allows more contact with the grandchildren. All people want respect and there's something to respect in most everybody. Concentrate on the positive things, congratulate them on their achievements — like remaining married when so many get divorced. Even small achievements count — like keeping a clean and neat house or a well-polished car. If the parents feel that you like and respect something about them they are more likely to take you up on your offer to baby-sit. Take the grandchildren for a weekend so the parents can get away or take the grandchildren on vacation with you, or during their school vacations.

RESCUING GRANDCHILDREN

Rescuing grandchildren requires real parenting and grandparenting talent, courage, determination and diplomacy. While the rescue rarely means that the grandparents physically take over the care of the child full time, it can. Sometimes only partial rescue is possible. You may be barred by circumstances from much direct personal contact with your grandchildren. The parents in troubled families may make it difficult for a grandparent to relate productively to the grandchild. Often the dysfunction is denied and the grandparent's efforts resisted. Good intentions are easily thwarted.

Luckily each child has up to four grandparents. If your efforts to help come to naught, perhaps one of the other grandparents has better relations with the parents and may be able to "adopt" the particular grandchild and serve some of his needs. So if your relations with the family create more tension than good, try to determine if one of the other grandparents is aware of the problems. Sometimes the two sets of grandparents may need to communicate, carefully, with each other to see that each child gets support. It may limit your own role with the child more than you would like, but it may assure support from at least one grandparent.

Some parents are so bad, so mixed up, that the grandparents sooner or later end up taking their grandchildren and raising them themselves. *Newsweek* magazine put out a special issue in which they told the story of skip-generation parent Ruth Rench. Ruth was looking forward to retirement and travel in five years. Then her three-year-old granddaughter told her that she had been molested by one of her mother's male friends. It was not the last time the girl would be abused. Rench wrote us that the Newsweek article covered only some of the many traumas suffered by her granddaughter; these led to her filing for custody.

Two years and $25,000 later, Rench, now 65, finally won custody of her granddaughter, who is now eight. She has joined a nationwide groundswell of grandparents who are stepping in to raise their children's children. Rench and her granddaughter are one of 95 "skip-generation" families who belong to the Ft. Worth area chapter of Grandparents Raising Grandchildren (GRG). Most of these grandparents are from good middle-class families who have never had to face anything like this before. They had to rescue their neglected or abused grandchildren from their parents or from foster homes. The parents become incompetent through the drug or alcohol abuse, mental problems, financial difficulty, or are so self-absorbed they lose control of themselves and their children. At the extreme, some mothers on drugs only want the child back so they can use the welfare payment to buy more drugs. Not surprisingly, the children suffering from such abusive parents do poorly in school, are antisocial and aggressive. Even when their grandparents take them, the children worry that grandma will abandon them. The grandparents who step in to save their grandchildren are described by *Newsweek* as "quietly heroic."

The trials and tribulations grandparents go through to help offer a counterpoint of hope for us all when we look at the appalling things some parents do to their children. The following incidents, and

Ruth Rench's story, were brought forward by the Fort Worth GRG group:

- The Miller's found their grandchildren, two-year old Nicole and fifteen-month old Cody hungry and unbathed in a rundown Oklahoma motel room. "Cody was like a little rabbit, he was so scared. . . And at two, Nicole had learned to change him and get his bottle because there was no one else to do it."

- A ten-year old girl, whose mother was an amphetamine addict serving a four-year prison term, wrote her mother, ". . . I have a lot of stuff to say to you but that's hard telling your mom that you don't want her out of jail. That's more harder than you think. . . If you die think of how [I] would feel because [I] said I hate you. . . . But mom, if you do go back on drugs if you get out don't call me or Grammy. . . ."

- Roseanne had to go to court because her daughter, on drugs, neglected and abused her grandson. But the judge felt like he had to give the mother another chance. Soon Rosanne was back in court again, with a picture of Jason, "Look at this. He's got handprints on his face. Look at his swollen eye. Look at his cut lip."

Reporter Al Martinez of the Los Angeles Times wrote, "There is probably no living creature more furious in defense of a blood relative than a grandmother protecting her grandchild. They roar like grizzlies. . ." He wrote of Grandmother Young whose thirteen-year-old grandson Tommy suffered brain damage from a five-day PCP drug induced coma. When her daughter-in-law began making it difficult to see Tommy, even though he was in a board-and-care home, Young "marched off to war." She helped get a bill passed which guaranteed visitation rights for grandparents.

- In Shreveport, Sara has cared for her grandson on and off since birth. The mother won custody of the baby in a divorce, but a year later she was beaten by a boyfriend and dumped on the family's front lawn. After recuperating she moved out, taking the baby. The baby later was sexually abused so the state assumed custody and now lets Sara take care of her grandson.

GRANDPARENTS RAISING GRANDCHILDREN

Grandparents understandably become quite angry with their adult children for dumping their grandchildren on them, often during retirement years and with no financial support. Instead there is a financial drain. Yet grandparents feel guilty if they don't help. They don't want to risk breaking up the family. But the problems grandparents face are formidable.

Grandparents Raising Grandchildren offers emotional support and political muscle to grandparents who for various reasons find themselves the primary care givers of their children's children. The Fort Worth GRG group explains their purposes and goals:

- To make the world a safer place for grandchildren whose only fault was to be born to parents who cannot or will not assume the responsibility of providing for the emotional support and well being of the child.

- To offer moral support to grandparents who find themselves the primary care givers of their grandchildren and to render assistance to fellow grandparents seeking guidance and advice in their efforts to protect and care for their minor grandchildren.

- To seek passage of legislation awarding qualified grandparents desirous of undertaking this responsibility the rights of care, custody and control of minor grandchildren in cases where the natural or custodial parents refuse or are unable to properly care for such child.

- To publicize and identify to the public and officers of the Judiciary, and any other persons involved in awarding legal custody of physically and mentally abused minor children, those cases and situations in which it would be in the best interest of the minor child to be placed in the care and custody of grandparents.

- To identify and work for the correction of situations that discriminate against the grandparents who are primary care givers of their grandchildren.

It is not easy to accomplish these goals. GRG explain, "Some of the difficulties facing grandparents who must rescue and care for their grandchildren either because of death, illness, drug or alcohol abuse, neglect or child abuse or simply because the parents no longer want the awesome task of caring for the children include:

- Many are looking forward to retirement and are not prepared to assume this responsibility and the emotional, physical and financial toll child-rearing takes.

- Many are in ill health, barely able to care for themselves.

- Many are angry and resentful at being forced into this role no matter what the circumstances. But they accept the role because of their love for their grandchildren and their sense of responsibility.

- Unfortunately, there is seldom a legal or formal custody agreement regarding the situation. The grandparents simply continue to love and care for the children — providing them with an education, health care, emotional support and a stable environment. However they face obstacles such as the difficulty of obtaining medical attention because they do not have formal custody:

  - Many insurance companies will not allow a grandparent to carry a grandchild as a dependent.

  - Many schools will not admit a child unless one parent is living with the grandparent.

  - Social Security benefits are not payable to a surviving primary care giver grandparent without adoption of the grandchild.

- Without legal custody, grandparents must give up their grandchildren to their children at any time without assurance that the child will be happy or well cared for. It doesn't matter if the natural parents are working or not, if they live in squalor, have little or no morals. A grandparent must literally fight their own children in court.

Yet as necessary as it is, the attempt to get custody can devastate relationships within the family and even result in the grandparents losing the grandchildren. It is not a step most grandparents take easily. Going public into court to try to prove your child is unfit is tough. But grandparents do it because they have to, and for most, it is the hardest thing they will ever do. All expenses and proof of responsibilities are required of the grandparents. Higher courts have ruled that it is the fundamental right of a parent to raise the children and current laws are less than kind to grandparents seeking custody of a grandchild even in the most serious conditions.

The Downside

One downside to utilizing the law to get a grandchild is that it may expose the child to increased family conflict. This speaks to the need to look out for the child's best interest which is usually not served by putting him in the middle of a loyalty struggle. Suing for visitation rights, for example, has to be weighed against the problems it may cause for the child. This indicates that very serious thought should be given to the idea, and possibly professional counseling sought, before going forward with such an action. Some grandparents may not be much better for their grandchildren than they were for their own children. Make certain that you are not the source of the dysfunction before you go too far in trying to "rescue" your grandchildren. Even if you are not dysfunctional, better ways may exist and should be explored. Sometimes, however, no choice exists and only the courts or welfare agencies can help you gain custody of your grandchild. But this step isn't taken lightly.

Barbara Kirkland, the Texas State President of Grandparents Raising Grandchildren, Inc., writes, "Grandparents know that the way the family codes are currently written they have about as much chance in court — even in the most severe cases — as a snow ball in Hell. They realize that if they proceed with [court] action they might not win and then could lose the child completely. With the present court system it is extremely difficult for a grandparent to win — so legal action is usually the last straw. As a result many, many children are just left with the grandparents until the natural parent decides to return, many years later in some cases, and assume their parenting role. Neither the grandparents nor the children can prevent the parent from waltzing in and picking up the children."

Sometimes Persistence Pays

In Long Island, New York, ten years ago two grandchildren lost their grandparents. Many things happened in the eight years it took to get them back: the children's mother left them, the father remarried and moved to another city and barred their maternal grandparents from seeing them, saying that it would upset them.

"We do not want to invade or intrude," said Edith Engel, the children's seventy-two-year-old grandmother, "we only want to help. . . Why should we let these kids think we too ran out on them? And you know how children are, they always think they did something wrong, that they are somehow to blame."

After many futile efforts to get the father to change his mind and allow them contact, the Engels finally took it to court — and lost. "Going to court is awful," said grandmother Engel. However they persisted in trying to reestablish their relationship with their grandchildren by writing letters to the father and having counselors mediate for them. They were finally reunited with their grandchildren who now, as teenagers, continue to visit and write.

WHEN YOU GET YOUR GRANDCHILD

How do you treat your abused grandchildren when you get them? First, of course, love them in a consistent, rational and authoritative way. They hunger for consistent unconditional love and reasonable safe limits. Reward them with the respect of truly listening to them. Offer them the solid dependable structure they did not get at home. Give them the opportunity and freedom to try new things. Demand good behavior and moderate your punishment by using neutral discipline. Let their problems be their own and offer suggestions about how they can solve them. Don't put up with bad behavior which will ultimately rebound on the child. But don't let their bad behavior get you upset. You can expect unusual reactions from children of dysfunctional parents. They need healing not scolding. Discipline with love. Rationally and calmly explain the possible consequences of their behavior and follow through with action to enforce the resulting reward or punishment. At the same time encourage them to do well. This says that you respect their ability and believe that they will become successful admirable people.

You may not feel able to assume an active parenting role if you were a dysfunctional parent when your children were young or if you grew up in a dysfunctional family; even if you feel bad about the way your own adult-child treats your grandchild. But the need for your help is still there and you have more going for you than you might think. In addition to taking parenting courses, if you grew up in a dysfunctional home yourself, you will have some strengths which normal parents may not have. Grandmother Jennie found that she enjoyed and benefited from a parenting course, even if it took awhile for her to find that she needed the help.

Sixty-nine-year-old Jennie was the only grandparent in the parenting class. It had started when Mrs. Brigham, Jerry's preschool teacher called her in for a conference. Mrs. Brigham had had a lot of opportunity to observe Jennie as well as Jerry. Parents at this preschool had to spend a day a week with their child at school. Jennie stayed every day! She became a real problem. The other mothers, young, reminded her of Jerry's mother and this stirred her up. She criticized them. She was a perfectionist, and wouldn't even let Jerry tie his shoes, "Because he is too sloppy!" During lunch hour she sat with Jerry and insisted that he eat every bite of his lunch. Her constant scowl intimidated the other children and even some of the teachers.

Mrs. Brigham, however, was not intimidated. She was a grand-mother herself. So she forthrightly told grandmother Jennie that she was being foolish, was interfering with Jerry's education and wasn't letting him grow up. Jennie's scowl turned to tears as she explained her fears that Jerry would turn out like his father and mother had — drug addicts who were killed, leaving grandmother to take the baby. Mrs. Brigham understood and empathized, and was able to comfort and convince Jennie that a better way could be found to avoid the errors made by Jerry's mom and dad. Mrs. Brigham even took Jennie to the first session of the YMCA parenting class. The class was an eye opener for Jennie, who learned of new ways to impart love and values as well as new ways to discipline. She began to give Jerry more freedom and found that he was able to take the responsibility for this freedom. Their relationship improved and Jerry became a much happier boy.

As she sipped coffee and comfortably exchanged small talk with the other parents on " graduation night," the last meeting of the parenting class, Jennie felt more content with herself than she had in years. Taking over the care of Jerry with the responsibility to raise him right had been frightening. Now that she was more sure of herself she could relax and begin to enjoy the experience.

SOME NEEDS OF CHILDREN OF DYSFUNCTIONAL PARENTS

Every child has talents, strengths and weaknesses. Some children seem innately strong enough to succeed in spite of alcoholic or drug ridden families, poverty or rejection by the parents. However, these children are often blessed with more than a favorable temperament. They frequently have positive relationships with other helping elders. Grandparents whose adult children are "dysfunctional" have a real opportunity to participate in helping a grandchild succeed educationally. One method involves taking a grandchild with you alone whenever possible. Expose him to positive experiences on vacations, for a whole summer or whenever the chance arises. Expose him to various facets of life which may draw out his interest. On the other hand don't just go to events or places that you like unless the child really likes them too. A quick dinner at McDonald's or Burger King may be better than a long (boring) one at an excellent French restaurant.

For some children, love alone seems to be their primary need. Lap time with grandmother may be the answer. This offers a feeling of security which the child may not get at home and it can have a major impact on his life. It gives him a grandparent figure to trust. Even if your grandchild lives away from you, point out to him that you are always as close as the telephone.

Most children learn best when they have the desire. Let them take the lead, take the initiative and make suggestions. This helps them develop their own powers. Don't try to overpower them with a schedule of things you insist on their doing. Talk with them about what they would like to do and the options available when they spend a week-end with you. Discuss upcoming vacations and give them some options if possible. Let them help with the planning. Above all keep the conversation away from the problems of their troubled parents as much as possible.

Children need to respect and love their parents — no matter how bad the parents may be. Try to dwell on the positive features of the child's life, and on the positive features of his parents. Don't make the mistake Thelma's grandmother did when she told Thelma that her mother was an alcoholic:

"Grandmother always seemed to criticize me. I remember her scolding me for not having my hair combed. There were other things, but I learned to ignore them. I think she really loved me — she had me over often and it was a relief to get away from home. Mom and Dad fought so often. And if Mom wasn't fighting with dad she sat around looking depressed. She had plenty of reason. Dad started hitting the bottle as soon as he got home, and usually he was already in his cups when he arrived. Sometimes he wouldn't come home at all for a few days. But he evidently supported us because we usually had enough to eat and clothes to wear. But the real trouble I had with grandmother started when I was seventeen. She told me that my mother was an alcoholic! I was furious, I hated her for that. I felt sorry for mother. She was treated so bad by Dad. Sometimes when they fought he would beat her up. If she drank some, I didn't blame her! I never liked Grandmother as well after that."

The truth hurts. Thelma's mother was an alcoholic. But she was all that Thelma had at home. Grandmother opened up Thelma's sorrow, insecurity, guilt and anger. Children of dysfunctional parents develop a delicate structure of defenses against the problems they live with. Often the defense is denial. For some, a skilled professional is needed to allow those defenses to come down without facing excessive hurt. Grandparents probably do more good by simply listening. Remember, a child's first loyalty will be to her parent. Don't close the door by criticizing those she loves. A sympathetic murmur rather than enthusiastic agreement about how bad the child's parents are may be more effective.

Children usually feel guilty about complaining about their parents, even if the parents deserve it. Don't aggravate this, because condemning the parents deepens the wound. Instead, agree by nods and gestures which indicate you are listening, you hear and understand — if the child wants to talk about it. Concentrate on the fact that the child did not cause the problem. Tell her the stories of some relatives or acquaintances who had the same problem, especially if they were able to get help and improve.

THE UNQUENCHABLE HUMAN SPIRIT

Examples of children who overcame the poor parenting they received and became solid, self-respecting upstanding citizens themselves can stimulate you and your grandchildren.

Barry

When Barry was nine years old his father left the family. Barry remembered how odd his father had acted, not at all like the other fathers in his midwestern town. Sometimes Dad almost seemed crazy with his talk about how he was going to buy a block of stores in the city, tear it down and build a skyscraper. He could hardly support the family and Barry once asked Dad where he would get the money; Dad said a bank would loan it to him. Sometimes he would stay up all night drawing his skyscraper. Other times he was depressed and just sat around the house, not even going to work at his job as a salesman in Grant's Emporium downtown. Barry was embarrassed by his father and didn't bring any friends home. The house was shabby. So when

Barry's dad just disappeared and never came back, it wasn't all that much of a loss to him.

No welfare agencies existed then. So Mother took in washing to keep food on the table. Barry, then at the age of nine, had to help support Mother and his two younger brothers. He helped Mr. Jones, the town mechanic, by cleaning up his shop on the week-ends. He discovered he was a good salesman when he tried to enlarge his paper route. Soon he was selling magazines too. The townspeople admired his energy and determination, as did the mayor whose admiration for Barry increased as Barry grew. In school Barry worked hard and excelled. The mayor, an ex-Army officer, suggested that Barry apply for West Point. Barry took the examinations and was awarded a Congressional appointment. Thirty years later Barry retired as a Brigadier General after successfully leading a regiment in the Korean War.

The human spirit is unquenchable. But in children it needs feeding; grandparents especially play a major role in feeding the spirit of the children of troubled parents. This requires enough dedication, wisdom and skills to make a diplomat's job look easy. The children may, like Barry, overcome adversity on their own, but even he had a helping hand from outside the family. In today's world children have trouble developing self-respect even if they can find work at an early age. The "security" of welfare tends to reduce a child's self-esteem and drive. This makes the role of grandparents even more important. Grandparents can build self-esteem by offering a structure, roots and emotional security that the state, no matter how well-intended, will never match. Grandparents are a bridge, offering the helping hand of ancestors and opening a way into a brighter future for children suffering under dysfunctional parents.

9   NEEDS OF CHILDREN

It seems redundant to say that many children today need more time from their parents than they get — however that ideal clashes with the realities of today and faces an increasing threat in the 1990s. Statistics vary, but by 1989 some 57% of mothers of preschoolers were in the work force full- or part-time. For single parents, usually divorced mothers, little choice exists. For many parents it takes two incomes to keep the household financially solvent. Many career oriented women believe that their contributions are greater in the workplace than the homeplace. Regardless, when both parents work 40 or more hours, travel 10 to 20 hours and sleep 56 hours a week, little time remains for all that a home requires. Bills must be paid, shopping and cooking done, and a plateful of other required necessities all reduce the amount of time parents have for the child.

The good news is that careful examination of the statistics by The Institute for American Values reveals that 44% of families with children under six years of age are fully traditional with father working and mother at home with the children. Another 16% of the mothers had part-time jobs rather than full time jobs. So 60% probably have enough time to meet their children's needs. For kids 14 to 17 years old at least 26% of the mothers are at home full time. But that leaves a lot of families who have trouble finding enough time for the children. And it raises the bothersome question of whether parents really need to spend as much time with their children as tradition dictates. The idea that quality time can make up for the small quantity of time spent with the child also requires careful observation. Meanwhile the alternatives are day care, after-school programs for latch key children or care by grandparents.

Why Did All The Parents Go?

Millions of mothers in the workplace help keep America prosperous. The two cars in every garage and two chickens in every pot promised by President Herbert Hoover in 1929 became a reality for most Americans by 1989. Unfortunately there may be no mother at home to cook the chickens or mother the kids. As grandparents we lived through the period where more and more mothers left home for work and left the childrearing to others. Why? Factors leading to this massive social change include Federal Income Tax policy, the relation between wages and inflation, American business needs, the pressure on women to "prove themselves" in the work place and the increase in labor saving devices for the home allowing more free time.

The $600 Federal Income Tax deduction allowed for each child in 1948, indirectly encouraged mothers to stay home and raise the children. Inflation and an inattentive Congress have wiped out the value of that deduction which, in today's dollars, would amount to $ 5600.00 per child! Both parents in large numbers of families have to work to keep up with inflation and satisfy the material aspects of the "good life". Most of today's women occupied significant niches in the workplace before they became mothers. Being used to living on two paychecks and facing the expenses of a new baby makes it difficult for them not to go right back to work. Meanwhile a labor-hungry American marketplace has become more and more dependent on the pool of intelligent and capable mothers to help them in their businesses.

Yet another factor adds to the pressure on mothers to seek employment outside the home. The woman's liberation movement, springing from many roots, tended to play down the worth of mothers at home in its effort to prove that women in the workplace and society are at least as good as men. In the process of adapting to all these social forces, the needs of children, the worth of mothering and the role of grandparents have largely been overlooked.

Recognizing these problems, coalitions of people and organizations have come together to educate and legislate in an attempt to make it possible for mothers to keep their jobs after a four month unpaid maternity leave. The business community, addicted to the relatively inexpensive and generally efficient woman labor force, resists the idea. America stands alone among the Industrialized Nations in lacking a social or economic policy which encourages or even allows mothers to stay at home with their children. In this mix-up of values, American business needs evidently take priority over the American baby's needs. Today's dollar appears more important than tomorrow's citizens. The unstated policy in the United States seems to be that they, and their needs, can be ignored.

Not all businesses ignore the needs of the family. The Rockford Institute Center on the Family in America Newsletter notes, ". . . the contemporary trend among corporations is simply to take over the private functions of the family, [offering] day-care, . . . diet and nutritional programs. Some writers even call on corporations to become the main teachers and transmitters of values in society." If this happened, what will it do to the American family and the children? The differences between this "business" concept and the full year of maternal leave at 90% of salary given in Sweden highlights some remarkable differences in values and assessment of relative worth.

When Mother Goes Off to Work

Like it or not, mothers working outside the home put preschoolers in day-care, and school age children in after school activities or care, or give the children a latch key so they can get into the house. Do these arrangements adequately substitute for the personal mothering needed by our children? Do many working parents manage to have enough time with their children? What quality of time, to say nothing of the amount, can exhausted parents provide? Certainly many children of working mothers seem to be doing well. Perhaps the quality of time these children receive is high enough to make up for the small amount of time their parents spend with them. Yet human nature hasn't changed. Children of today need the basics just as we did when we were children. Not only for food, clothes, housing and education, but for mothering — for enough time for each child to enable mother to recognize and treat him as the unique individual he is.

Nearly every parent has gone through the experience of puzzling out the different personalities of each of their children. Generally the child's own parents and grandparents have the drive, dedication, motivation and empathy to consider and treat each particular child in the most effective way, to personalize care. But drive and empathy aside, the effort takes personal time with the child, getting to know him.

Each child needs personal individual care and thought if she is to develop to her full potential. In the past in America, and currently in Asia, recognizing and coping with this uniqueness was mostly the role of mother backed up by grandparents in the extended family. They recognized how different children are from each other. We are not like a pure bred strain of dogs. Recognition of this variability while dealing with individual people, even little people, becomes a must. Children require consideration and treatment as individuals. Do they get it?

This is the day of mass education, of mass merchandising and of mass exposure to the values taught by television. We also live in a time of "mass" day-care. Who gives this care and what are their qualifications? Few have formal training and not many have a degree in child development, for day care jobs pay minimum wages. If they do have a degree they tend to bring a standardized approach to children. Those uneducated in child rearing, except by the way they were raised and by their own experiences, each has his or her own "standard" approach. By contrast our own children share enough individual genetic traits with each parent or grandparent that we usually recognize the special significance of their feelings and actions which would escape a stranger. Often we understand the way they think or feel about things because we experienced the same reactions ourselves. Even so it takes a lot of parental time, effort and dedication to really sort out each child's individual make up enough to be able to handle him well.

Grandparents Call It Love

Another key need of children is for what researchers call attachment or bonding. Most grandparents call it love. We do become attached to our children and our grandchildren. If we don't, the unloved, unattached child develops some very serious problems. The need for love and nurturing starts at birth. But, as we have seen, the business community wants mothers back on the job as early as possible. As a result mothers are expected to return to their jobs just four to six weeks after delivery. No matter that they have just gone through pregnancy, labor and delivery, have a low hormone level and are still getting up at night feeding the baby. The boss wants them back.

Pediatrician T. Berry Brazelton spearheads the efforts to get maternity leave for mothers. He cites compelling evidence that at least four months is needed to assure maximum bonding and the development of trust in the infant. Research work in this area of child-rearing goes all the way back to studies on infants raised in foundling homes without handling or loving attention; they often died. Mary Ainsworth, whose research was regarded as a breakthrough in the 1960s, demonstrated that the attachment pattern formed in infancy persists. Preschoolers who lacked adequate mothering in infancy have poor peer relationships, avoid problem solving, lack self-confidence and sometimes exhibit a sense of hopelessness. Research by Jay Belsky leads him to advise that problems may occur if a baby is in substitute care for more than 20 hours a week. Others note that a large proportion of delinquent boys suffered early maternal separation. Researcher Ainsworth holds that, "We don't know how the quality of day-care affects attachment outcomes, how many kids are really at risk — or whether a mother who stays home bored and resentful is better than one who comes home happy and fulfilled." Still, her mentor and co-worker John Bowbly noted that, "We have ample evidence that certain types of experience in childhood are risk factors."

Pediatricians have observed for decades the anxieties created by repeated changes of care takers during the first year of life. Research done at the Harvard Preschool Project and confirmed in practice by the Parents As Teachers program of the Missouri public school system, demonstrated the need for a readily available mother during the first three years of life. Toddlers getting enthusiastic responses for their developmental steps, who are able to follow Mother around and usually get her help when they want it, develop better language skills and intellectual ability than other infants kept isolated in playpens with educational toys. Those infants who developed best had Mother available much more of the time. In day-care it is not uncommon to have six infants or twelve toddlers with one care taker, and the turnover of workers in day-care is very high.

Burton White, in *Educating the Infant and Toddler* asks how even an experienced day-care provider can respond to the baby's first step as enthusiastically as the baby's mother. After all, she has seen 100 babies take their first steps. Perhaps equally important is the sense of loss felt by parents who have so little time to spend with their children, to watch and help them develop. Television producer Rhonda Arnold found this out:

"One day when my baby was about a year old I came home and the sitter beamed, 'I almost called to tell you he walked today'

"The trouble was, my baby was growing up with me as an onlooker. I was known in the world of TV. I'd walk into a restaurant and people would nod but when I came home my son cried. He reached for his baby sitter."

One negative that no one denies is that putting large numbers of infants and preschoolers with immature immune systems into day-care increases the number of illnesses. Day-care has been aptly described as a "bug factory" because of the great increase in bacterial, viral and parasitic infections it creates. Children in these units not only have a high incidence of infection, they bring these infections home and spread them, via their brothers, sisters and parents to school and the work force. However the bulk of the negatives involve the effects on the children's psychological development which will outlast the effects of most illness.

Preschoolers and Up

The problems faced by children of working mothers continues beyond the first three years. Many preschoolers in day-care do very well — but others have difficulties. At a time when children should feel that the world is theirs to grab, that their importance is validated by Mothers availability, they are instead placed in a large group of immature kids most of their waking time. Don't misunderstand, the preschooler needs to learn to get along with other children and for this reason part-time nursery school is very worthwhile. But some full-time day-care preschoolers can develop undesirable traits.

Elizabeth Wolf, a San Diego kindergarten teacher, in her book *Meanwhile Back to The Children,* sees day-care as a negative experience for children:

"Children, in the formative years of their lives, need continual direction, support, and encouragement from the significant persons in their lives — namely their parents. Their basic needs have not changed. They will *always* need warm, loving unhurried care from their parents in a non-threatening situation, in order to develop normally as a well-adjusted personality. When the needs are not met satisfactorily in the home (one of the foremost problems of our unstable home situation today), children 'act out' their frustrations through their attitudes, their expressions and their actions. It is these actions I see in the classroom that disturb me the most. . . Day-care works in direct opposition to the basic needs of the young child entering school by the very virtue of their size, approximately 120 children. They create an unhealthy atmosphere for growing children."

She maintains, as do others, that children crammed together in large groups for long periods of time, begin to develop antisocial patterns. The result is that they take out their frustrations on one another in violent ways. They develop cliques before kindergarten, a common bond and almost an inmate mentality. Wolfe continues:

"Has society gone mad when its well intentioned but ill conceived ideas. . . result in little children acting out their frustrations on each other in such a violent way? These children are trying to tell us something. They're trying to say that they don't like being institutionalized in a massive group situation. They're trying to tell us that they too need some peace and quiet in their lives just like adults. When are we going to start listening to them?" Children require privacy too!

The problems created by starting toddlers in large preschool day-care institutions bothers many kindergarten teachers. It also bothers a lot of pediatricians when parents bring a six-week-old baby to the office for an illness saying that he caught it in "school." Parents use the term "school" to assuage their guilt feelings about abandoning their infant to day care.

Intergenerational Day-Care; One Solution

Steven W. Brummel, president of the Elvirita Lewis Foundation, offers the concept of intergenerational day-care to help meet the needs of grandparents as well as children. Grandparents who go out of retirement and go to work in day-care centers serve as more than just a baby sitter and diaper changer. They bring a lot of wisdom, empathy, experience and emotional control to the job. Their values have an effect. They are more supportive and patient than many of the teenagers employed in day-care, are more respected and tend to calm the children. Older workers have a lower turnover rate than most day-care workers and thus offer more continuity and stability for the children. Many grandparents find the work emotionally rewarding as well as financially helpful. This is a practical and altruistic solution well worth considering for "retired" grandparents.

School's Out and Nobody's Home!

But what about school, say, after kindergarten? Isn't it reasonable for a mother to work outside the home when her child spends most of the day in school? If so, what do you do with the child when school's out and nobody's home? The National Committee for Prevention of Child Abuse reported on a 1985 national conference on latchkey children. Barbara D. Finberg of the Carnegie Corporation of New York wrote in the foreword of the report:

"These children at home – or on the street – are often reported to be fearful, lonely, and immobile before a television set; but they may be confident, happily independent, and engaged in rewarding activity. Aside from their mental states, though, children alone are more vulnerable to physical danger: accidents, sexual abuse, and experimentation with alcohol, tobacco, and drugs can all occur more easily when an adult is not present. To protect their children, parents often do not permit them to invite other children into their homes when parents are absent. Neither can they provide transportation or accompany their children to a Scout or recreation group or special lessons. Children home alone, therefore, even if safe and unafraid, may be missing many opportunities to develop interests, talents, and personal skills that would enrich, perhaps even shape, their futures."

Joan Bergstrom, of Wheelock College's Department of Professional Studies in early childhood, emphasized the opportunities for children in middle childhood:

"These years (age six to twelve) are rich with possibilities. They are the time when the critical foundation is laid for adolescence and beyond. During these years children learn to interpret the world. When the children reach the age of six they are receptive; their eagerness and ability to learn are at a high level. But the clock is ticking. As children leave this stage, their thoughts turn inward toward their own identities, and their receptivity to new experiences is diminished. These six years, then, are to be treasured."

Many of the contributors to this conference about latch key children worried about the parent's feelings of guilt and inadequacy. They rejected the terms latchkey children or unsupervised children because of "negative connotations." Some thought the "self-care" label best described the situation.

The experts at the conference came up with positive recommendations by which "children can experience a rich and rewarding childhood." It is of more than passing interest to grandparents that some programs offered as partial solutions involved grandparents. For example, Age Link in North Carolina brings in people over 65 to share their skills, crafts and storytelling. Another good model is the Kid's Place program in Seattle where children's concepts and ideas are valued and positive projects help fill the void created by absent parents. This program will be discussed more fully later. But some observers saw a devaluation of childhood with many parents acting as if they believe they cannot afford childhood for their children.

Teenagers

Adolescents especially need supervision and attention to keep them off drugs and alcohol and away from premature sexual activities or sexual abuse. In their attempt to grow up, to be adult, they usually push the limits and rebel against traditional family values. Their impulsive behavior makes them susceptible to the values of their peers. Those lacking confidence in their own worth become especially susceptible. If their friends taunt them for not trying a drug they may not have the strength to say "No." Drug abuse by teenagers of rational-authoritative parents was half that of teenagers of authoritarian or permissive parents. A survey in Southern California of 5000 teenagers revealed that twice as many kids whose mothers were not at home abused drugs. The incidence is undoubtedly higher among adolescents with drug abusing parents.

If a relative, or even a stranger whom the children feel respects and values them, tries to sexually molest a child he or she may succumb without a second thought. The sex urge exists, especially in adolescents, as does the tendency to experiment. Even younger children are susceptible to adult attention and will trade sexual favors for it. Take the court records of 41-year old Charles who estimated that he had molested sixty children: He said, "I find these kids from unhappy homes. And I have a way of becoming friends with kids immediately. I'll listen to them when they want to talk, all the things their parents won't do. . . I like having sex when I want it, being in complete control of the situation."

Are There Ways Out?

However, when mother cannot be home, and many can't, then what? Are there other options? Discussion about day-care tends to become emotional because of the strong feelings involved. Some defenders of day-care point to cases of inept mothers whose children are better off in someone else's care, or see mothering at home as a dull unchallenging occupation that stifles the creativity of women. Some mothers do look on work outside the home as a method of saving their sanity and self-esteem. Many career-pursuing mothers consider themselves capable of doing both jobs well.

Citing projections that by 1990, 70% of all mothers of children age 6 to 17 will be in the labor force at least part time, psychology professor Edward F. Zigler of Yale came up with a model for a 21st Century School. *Parent's Magazine* reported that in a Missouri school where the model is being tried out, that seven-year-old Austin Miller spends nearly 10 hours there and often doesn't want to go home at the end of the day. His parents were reportedly thrilled. Before and after regular school his activities are under the direction of trained day-care workers who allow considerable freedom and choices of activities that include caring for pets, afternoon snacks and playing with friends. The school also offers information and referrals for parents, home visits for new parents, training for neighborhood day-care providers, and day-care in the school for three to four-year-olds.

David Elkind in his book, *Grandparenting*, wrote, "For hurried, stressed parents, the image of the sophisticated, self-assured, independent child ready to take on whatever life has to offer is appealing. Children and youth may come to believe it as well. This places great stress upon young people because they really are not instant adults."

The concept of university-trained experts overseeing day-care sounds attractive. However Meryl Frank, who ran a Yale University program that studied the issue of parental leave after giving birth, found she was a novice when she tried to find someone to watch her five-month-old baby. *Newsweek* reported that she changed child-care arrangements nine times over the next two years for a variety of reasons including lack of attention by day-care workers, non-English speaking baby sitters, and harsh nannies. She found poor student/staff ratios and very high turnover rates of personnel. Others point out that so far chain franchised day care centers don't do well because of lapses in quality.

Solutions?

Not all children in day-care suffer neglect and many latchkey children in safe suburbs do well. Peter Coolsen of the National Committee for prevention of child abuse reported that being on one's own after school *can* be a growth inducing challenge — it tells the child he is big enough and smart enough to take care of himself. But it is obvious that many children, if not most, would benefit from grandparenting. Real opportunity exists for grandparents to meet children's needs in these circumstances.

Ways Grandparents Can Help

In our pluralistic American society several ways out of the day-care/latch-key/parent guilt dilemma exist. Whatever the option, grandparents should get involved and help forge solutions. In some families Mother stays home and material expectations are reduced. In these circumstances, well-to-do grandparents can help by giving presents, taking the family on vacations, or buying the children's clothes. Meanwhile, more and more mothers supplement the family income by taking jobs where they can work at home. Or mother and father take opposite shifts at work and "pass each other in the night" so one will be home during the day and the other in the evening. Grandparents can give these parents a break, allowing them some time alone together, by taking a turn with the kids. More thought is being given to the suggestion that Federal and State income tax policy should encourage part-time rather than full-time work for mothers with children at home. We grandparents can help push such concepts.

Mothers who do stay at home with their children have formed organizations like Mothers At Home and Kids First to enhance the morale of stay-at-home mothers and to educate the public, and in some cases to politically emphasize the need of children for mothers at home. Given the choice, over half of working mothers would rather be home with their children. Surveys have shown that mothers who stay home are generally satisfied.

Feeling Guilty?

The temptation exists to blame many of today's social and personal ills on the lack of parenting received by a lot of American children. Certainly some of these problems can be blamed on the lack of parenting time. Experts disagree, but if pressed for an answer, many of those who sanction working mothers do so because they feel that increasing maternal guilt is an unhealthy approach to the problem. Increasing maternal guilt, they point out, may create resentment toward the children. Other experts, skeptical and academically bent, point to the lack of scientific proof that mothers who work thereby damage their children.

The bottom line is this: What is day-care going to do to the kids in the future? Some researchers say there is no clear evidence that day-care places an infant at risk. Others seem reluctant to publicly discuss the problems for fear of making working parents feel that they are bad parents. The guilt issue also bothers many grandparents. One grandfather, after reading some of this material, complained, "The general feeling is that I am having a guilt trip laid on me for not taking a more active role with my own grandchildren. The main reason I don't is geography."

Guilt is the evolutionary handmaiden of parenting and grand-parenting. If no guilt was felt some might easily abandon their children and grandchildren. Underneath it all even parents who do an exceptional job usually have some guilt feelings. At least one person apparently feels that parents don't feel guilty enough. Donald E. Greydanus, M.D., a concerned Iowa physician wrote in the American Medical

Association News, "Many parents spend endless hours at their profession but relatively few precious minutes with their children. In some families where both parents are working, the children spend much of their time and learn much of their life experiences from non-parent figures. . . We seem content to allow TV and peers to be the main teachers of our children regarding sexuality education and violence appreciation. As adults seem more preoccupied with themselves and less concerned with their children, we see growing problems in our offspring. These children seem to be developing even greater difficulties with depression, substance abuse, runaway behavior. . ."

The stakes are high for future adults. Psychiatrist Karl Meninger said "The most important job a parent can undertake is giving his or her child a proper childhood. People repeat in adult life emotions they experienced in childhood. Many of the people who I spent the last thirty to forty years treating at so much per minute wouldn't have needed any treatment at all if they had the right care as children."

Where Grandparents Come In

Your own grandchildren may have a desperate but hidden need to be either taken out of the crowd or to be given good adult guidance when home. If they are too far away for you to help them, you can at least help others. Many opportunities exist in your neighborhood or community to volunteer to help other children. Even being a school crossing guard who greets and comes to know the children can have a positive effect. If your community has no good programs you can write to Kid'sPlace for ideas. Grandparents, seniors, can find many ways to help America's children.

We started this chapter with the question of whether parents need to spend as much time with their children as tradition dictates. Admitting that we cannot be certain, enough evidence has accumulated to indicate that increasing difficulties occur if not enough parental time is spent with growing children. Will these problems last into adult life? The need of an infant and child for strong parental attachment, for continuity of personal nurturing and control, cannot be overemphasized. If they can't attach firmly to Mother or Grandmother, who *can* they attach to? Yet many mothers have to work to survive, economically or psychologically. Their children especially have an urgent need for their grandparents and extended family to get back into the picture. Grandparents can and do offer continuity and attachment. They can and do make a better life for their grandchildren — and youth in general. Life takes on more zest and greater meaning when we help the young and contribute to the future. It completes our life cycle and vindicates our existence, if that needs vindication. It makes us more content.

CHILDREN WITH DISEASES

Many children need extra help because of their medical problems. The list of conditions which disable children is intimidating. They run from failure to grow well because of cystic fibrosis or hypothyroidism to premature aging of children with progeria, or from mental retardation to epilepsy. Here we will present two new diseases and the classic conditions of diabetes and retardation as examples of how grandparents can help.

AIDS and "Crack" babies

Modern society suffers from the effects of "modern" new and terrifying illness AIDS, caused by the HIV virus. This lethal infection is transmitted to newly born infants from their mothers during pregnancy or to children with hemophilia from the transfusion of blood factors. The rate of infection in newborns is growing rapidly, creating anxiety among all levels of society, particularly among the parents and grandparents. Fortunately babies and children with AIDS can be loved and carefully cared for without significant risk of contracting the disease. It is spread by blood and semen, both of which are unlikely to come from infants.

At the same time the epidemic of "crack" afflicts society and its newborns. Pregnant mothers who use cocaine severely damage their babies who had no choice in the matter. Those who survive have awful times before the acute effects of the drug wear off. They cry incessantly, are hyperactive or often rigid and cannot be comforted in the usual way. It appears that many suffer significant brain damage. Hospital personnel who care for these babies become as stressed as the parents. Help is needed.

The plight of crack babies has touched a nerve in society and grandparents, among others, are volunteering in startling numbers to help these innocents. They need the calm and the quiet touch grandparents have, often just being held close and rocked in a darkened room, to help them "come down" from their enforced in-utero addiction. The San Francisco Examiner reported that grandmother Jeanie Hunter volunteers at Children's Hospital — during her lunch hour — to give love and attention to crack babies. She knows that these infants need special attention that the doctors and nurses do not have time to give.

In an earlier chapter we discussed the need for grandmothers to counsel their daughters and daughters-in-law about their pregnancies. Grandmothers are especially listened to during the first pregnancy and have an opportunity to set a high standard of conduct. If nothing else, grandmothers can stress two essentials, prenatal care and avoidance of alcohol and drugs. Whatever bit of that advice is taken pays off in healthier newborns with a better opportunity in life. Grandparents can make the difference between success and failure as the nation faces these new epidemics. They can also be of great value to families when the grandchild comes down with a chronic disease like diabetes.

Diabetics

Children are usually thrilled to have their grandparents all to themselves, to have their undivided attention. That occurs at a special camp for diabetic children and their grandparents run by Dr. Joan MacCracken, a Bangor Maine pediatric endocrinologist and Patricia Stenger, R.N., camp director. They both feel that the Camp Grand concept, which is spreading to other parts of the country, is a great way to help these children and their families. Stenger wrote:

"For grandparents the initial reaction to the news that a grandchild has diabetes can be panic. One grandmother said, "It was devastating. All of a sudden I felt like I had lost her." MacCracken and Stenger know that, instead, becoming involved can make the grandparent/grandchild bond even stronger. This does require education about diabetes. But it takes more than that. Stenger wrote:

"You now have a double role. You are not only concerned about the newly diagnosed grandchild, but you are involved with your own children who have to face this crisis. Sometimes you may become the source of strength for the family, a place for a grieving son or daughter and his or her spouse to go to when they are at the end of their rope, a shoulder they can cry on. You may also step in as caretaker for the other children in the family. The youngsters without diabetes will need a close, reassuring family member to be with them while their parents are spending long hours at the hospital.

"But what happens to your long-term role now that your grandchild had been diagnosed with diabetes? The answer to many of your concerns lies in one word — education. Although grandparents may be asked to give support and practical help, usually they are left out of the diabetes education process. If you're not clear what this illness is, if you don't understand why there are difficulties with blood-sugar control or how to handle it, get involved in diabetes education.

"If you are not knowledgeable about diabetes treatment, the child's parents will probably be reluctant to leave him or her with you for long periods of time. Worse, you may fear your own ability to care for your grandchild with diabetes. The fact is, diabetes is a complex disease, and can be terribly frightening if you know nothing about it. It would be difficult for you to spend much time taking care of a child with diabetes if you didn't know anything about insulin shots, blood-glucose monitoring, or low blood sugar.

"It's worrisome if you aren't sure whether there's a substitute for the chocolate chip cookies you used to make together. So ask to be included in the education process, or pursue it on your own. See whether you can accompany the child or the child and parent to doctor's appointments. Ask to go along to support group meetings, clinics, and diabetes education programs. Or, locate these resources for yourself. You'll find free classes through your local ADA chapter. The American Diabetes Association also has a great deal of printed information available. There are many books and magazine articles on diabetes.

"Fortified by the knowledge of the revolutionary advances in treatment you will be able to understand the relationship between insulin and the chocolate chip cookies your grandson loves. His parents will feel comfortable letting him stay with you or go on a trip with you — and you will feel comfortable having him around. As one grandmother said, "This makes me feel trusted and loved.""

Retardation and Birth Defects

Other problems such as mental retardation from Down's Syndrome, or brain damage from infectious disease or injury are not rare. When children are affected by any of these conditions family dynamics are altered, often bringing the grandparents into a closer relationship as the family rallies around the child to meet his needs. A wide variety of birth defects create lifelong needs for medical and psychological care and pose major financial and social difficulties for parents. Grandparents can help tremendously with emotional support, personal attention and finances. Grandparents can be invaluable and appreciated beyond belief for spelling the parents, taking the child for appointments in clinics or rehabilitation centers. In this way they play a highly significant role in the child's world and strengthen the family as it meets the challenge of the disability.

Becoming educated about your grandchild's handicap, whatever it is, is essential to your being able to provide appropriate and meaningful support.

Special Educational Needs

Today's parents, frequently both working, often lack the time they need to help a child out of academic difficulties. The children of single parents do not do as well in school as children in intact families. Grandparents can help meet the academic needs of their grandchildren in many ways. First, by avoiding any implication that the problems spring from parental actions or attitudes. Probably the parents already feel guilty and are usually oversensitive to any perceived accusations. Sometimes grandparents may be able to help financially with tutors or special schools. For working parents the grandparents availability and willingness to take the child to sessions with tutors, psychologists or for pediatric examinations or counseling is a great help. At all times a grandparent's warm and friendly optimism and support for the child helps. This gives the child a sense of belonging, of being wanted, of being important enough to warrant the extra efforts involved.

Most grandparents can establish a comfortable relationship with their families and become a significant participant in the grandchildren's lives. Generally the role involves some parenting, or rather, grandparenting functions. This role of offering support and help becomes very important, especially if a grandchild's academic or social development sputters.

Your effectiveness in helping depends to a great deal upon your relationship with your grandchild's parents. As we noted, even in families with problems, a grandparent can have at least some effect. But if your child and son-in-law or daughter-in-law agree, you can become a major additional resource to your child's academic development. Even if they don't want you "meddling," opportunities still exist to help with subtle guidance, motivation and modeling — although you do have to be careful and diplomatic or you may find that the parent, like Cherie, gets upset at your attempts to help.

Cherie

Cherie, a somewhat hyperactive young mother, discussing her child's learning difficulties with the pediatrician, complained, "When we went to Mom's, she had laid out some brochures on special schools. It sort of made me mad. I want to make the decision about what to do about Tim and his learning problems myself."

Perhaps Cherie's parents tried to be a bit too subtle and might have gotten further if they had openly asked if they could help and then offered financial support. Usually it pays to be available, offer help and let the parents take the lead. Meanwhile it doesn't hurt to study. Your effectiveness in helping your adult-child and spouse with your grandchild's learning problems will increase with your understanding of normal childhood intellectual and developmental steps and signs of problems that can lead to failure. Many areas of development are involved — learning, school success, social popularity, effectiveness and self-esteem.

The issue of self-esteem has led to programs in schools to boost self-confidence in an effort to fill the void left by full-time working parents, the splintered family network and family troubles. Social scientists say that many students come to class lacking the emotional strengths they need to master academic subjects. Dean Leonard Schneiderman of the School of Social Welfare at the University of California in Los Angeles wrote, "We have increasing demand on the schools to compensate for what is lacking in families." One major lack is the grandparent.

Practical Ways of Helping

Good teachers recognize that their role requires the use of power. But today's teachers, in many instances, may even lack the ability to keep a class orderly and quiet. Many children waste their powers by disrupting class, pressing the teacher's button, or becoming the class clown. This helps them avoid the feeling of boredom and helplessness which exist when learning comes hard. One of the first things grandparents can accomplish is to elevate the prestige of teachers in general. Start by showing respect for teachers.

The tone of respect in day-to-day conversations whenever talking about teachers raises their image in the minds of children. Talking about good teachers increases a child's willingness to try to learn, to look for the good in teachers. While poor teachers exist, don't let conversations dwell on them. Instead, say, "Never let a teacher stand between you and an education." Children doing poorly often want to blame their problems on their teachers. Avoid the trap of sympathy unless you are certain the teacher is really ineffective. Instead, offer to help the grandchild understand the subject. For example, if Johnny is struggling with French, offer a funny phrase or joke in French. Sprinkle a few French phrases in your conversation. Memorize a few and try them out on him. Even make fun of yourself, of the way you probably mispronounce the words. If he responds, be impressed by whatever he has learned. Make it fun.

Some children have trouble reading. Part of the problem may stem from the different methods teachers use. Not all children respond to any one method. The rote memory method of repetition of "See Spot Run" bores many children to exhaustion. It would us too, if we had to read those insipid books. In place of rote memory, the phonics technique enables children to read most words by memorizing the look and sounds of 107 letter combinations. This allows the letter symbols to be translated into sound and speech opening the child's auditory memory banks so he can coordinate the written work with the words he hears. One grandmother taught her granddaughter how to read during a week's vacation with her, using a book which shows how to teach phonics at home.

Some children have auditory memory problems and difficulties understanding words. Some have visual-neural difficulties which make it difficult for them to understand the symbols we call letters and words. A few even need to feel individual letters with their fingers to enable them to appreciate the differences. Children with reading difficulties often deserve to be studied by educational specialists to determine how best to proceed. To discover whether or not your grandchild has problems may require tact. You certainly don't want to start by criticizing if you want to help. Your attitude, when you offer to help, is probably more important than your direct knowledge of the subject. Yet you may be aware that reading difficulties run in the family and thus be able to offer some helpful background.

If you are in a position to work directly with the child, don't try to overpower him with demands. Instead, if the family rules say no play until homework is done, offer to help so the two of you can go to the playground. Then make learning enjoyable, a game with laughs and rewards. For example, if eight-year-old Johnny has trouble learning to multiply 8 times 7, help him with the answer and then say, "Let's say 8 times 7 is 56 twenty times on the way to the park. Then when we get there, should I buy you 56 ice cream cones, or 7 or 8?" When you get there, laugh and say, "Gosh Johnny, I don't have enough money and you don't have enough room for 56 ice cream cones or even 7 or 8. I guess we will have to settle for one rather than 56. O.K.?"

Perhaps the first step toward discovering your grandchild's academic status involves enthusiastic interest in his school. Have him take you to his school and point out his class room. Mix some play with the visit and give him an opportunity to show you how well he reads. Most grammar school classrooms have words up on the board visible through the window. Bring him a book appropriate to his interests and age. If baseball constitutes his life, bring a book on baseball. Offer to help him read it if it seems too hard. Maybe when the book is finished you can go see a game. Or ask if he will read a little of it to you as you left your glasses home. Help him only if he asks for help; don't criticize his lack of skills. Instead, look for his strengths and weaknesses. Praise his strengths and mentally note his weaknesses.

Many children have no speech or reading problems until they reach an age when certain language skills should develop. This can occur as late as junior high school. Then their brain "computer screen" may not be large enough to cope with all the demands placed on it. Some have trouble developing an adequate vocabulary. Others are confused by words having several meanings. Grandparents can help by using a variety of words in conversation and story telling.

Children with language problems often become humiliated losers in school and quit trying or rebel. Overburdened teachers and overburdened working parents may not have enough time or energy to help the child. Children can suffer more from learning difficulties than from pneumonia. A helping hand from grandparents, directly or indirectly, may be lifesaving. Diplomacy and tact are required to get the parents and the child to accept help. Sometimes the child requires extensive study by learning disability experts, and grandparents might be able to help financially. It also can help to tell the story of great uncle Jake who had the same problem and learned to compensate and became a success in life. Emphasize what Jake had to do to compensate and how he went about getting help and helping himself.

THE NEED FOR SOCIAL DEVELOPMENT

Some grandchildren are a pain to be around, especially the child who ignores rules and lacks self-control. Some of these children, especially in middle childhood, have hidden learning disabilities which cause their problems. They may have difficulty in relating to other people. Sometimes this appears at an early age in the form of hyper-activity or inability to concentrate. Often they do not understand the effect of their actions on others. They may get by in an accepting family only to have difficulty in dealing with children outside the family. Some children have never pleased the adults in their world, possibly because of learning problems, and therefore may become involved in gangs where they find some approval for their antisocial activities. The grandparent's warm acceptance of a child, no matter what his failings and disabilities are, may reduce that child's tendency to become involved in gangs.

Things which go wrong with proper socialization are legion. Grandparents may note that a particular child's personality clashes with Mother's or Father's. These children need an out, another parent figure who understands their feelings and shows them ways to cope. Children with attention deficits or impulsive behavior often turn people off.

Some children with language problems also turn off people. Unpopular children, for whatever cause, can often be spotted because they have no friends or only have younger children for friends. Grandparents, by experience, may be able to help a child's social development and popularity skills. First by love and unconditional support. The grandparent may be the only one offering such support and becomes a beacon and source of strength and comfort to a child who might otherwise be completely rejected, lonely and hurting. One can, by quietly observing the child and recognizing the signs and symptoms of social maldevelopment, help the child learn to develop better strategies to cope with his problems. The following table offers a summary of skills children need to develop popularity.

CRITICAL POPULARITY SKILLS*

- Learning to perceive and interpret the feeling and drift of a social situation before entering and acting.
- Learning to really recognize and understand other people and make them feel wanted and important.
- Learning how to diplomatically resolve conflict without aggression.
- Learning to change their language to fit with the group.
- Developing the ability to show their own feelings accurately.
- Learning to understand how others react to their statements and actions.
- Learning to "market" themselves.
- Learning how to listen to others and verbally and non-verbally demonstrate their understanding.
- Learning to avoid viewing and judging people as unchanging and predictable.
- Learning the significance of loyalty in friendship.
- Acquiring moral values.

---

*Adapted from *Social Development in Middle Childhood*, Adrian Sandler, M.D., Pediatric Annals, June 1989.

A Positive Future

In the process of finding and labeling the problem, and developing strategies and techniques to help the child solve his problem, the child's self-esteem must be protected. Areas of strengths should be emphasized. A positive future for the child should be anticipated and projected by all involved with him. If the family's standard expectations for the child appear to be unreachable, alternative paths for the child should be suggested and encouraged. Some children have no interest or talent for college, yet have fine mechanical skills and will make great mechanics.

Grandparents can often help directly if the parents willingly invite them to be part of the team. If not, they can help by moral support and a positive attitude toward the child. In subtle ways the grandparents may help by modeling, by "historical" stories offered about people who managed in spite of similar deficiencies, and by making learning fun and rewarding rather than dull and boring. In summary, a grandparent's love is irreplaceable and may be put to good use in helping grandchildren develop academic and social competence.

10 HOMES, NEIGHBORHOODS AND COMMUNITIES
What Our Grandchildren Need

A Place to Live

Children and their families need a place to live that includes more than four walls to protect against the elements. Within those four walls the toddler requires a safe world to explore, the preschooler a place to play and the school-age child a stimulating friendly environment with books, maps, music and a place to be alone. Home should include an uncrowded view from the windows offering a needed sense of space. Home includes safe yards, places to run and play, a place with a sense of freedom and some open horizons.

Home is where the heart is. The very personal treasures in the home, from furnishings and pictures to toys and books, reflect the families interests and values. In times gone by, the country doctor making a house call could tell a lot about his patient by simply being a good observer of the home. Similarly today, an architect designing a house for a client will ask to spend some time at the client's home to see how they live. He will also walk around the neighborhood to take the area into account in his plans. He may even ask about the extended family, where grandfather and grandmother live and how often they visit or stay over.

Where the grandparents choose to live plays a role in the kind of relationship they have with their grandchildren. Some choose to live in retirement homes or villages, where they are among their own generation and the children's visits are brief. Others continue to live where they raised their children and are comfortable in these familiar surroundings. Whatever the location, Grandma and Grandpa's house is usually very different from the grandchildren's own home. Children enjoy exploring the intriguing things collected by Grandma and Grandpa and hearing the fascinating stories that go with them.

Civilized Visits to Grandmother's Home

Some grandmothers and grandfathers find that the grandchildren's visits are catastrophes; they leave a trail of strewn toys and disorder. Undisciplined and untidy, they may also be uncaring about grandparents prize possessions. The real little ones seem to gobble up everything in their paths.

Of course grandparents have to be realistic about the normal stage of development of the child. Crawling babies and toddlers cannot be expected to leave things alone. They are programmed by nature, not by parents, to explore. At first everything has to go into the mouth. They have been described as being grazing animals — they have to taste the world. This stage is especially dangerous for they are very apt to poison themselves by eating grandfather's pills or getting under the sink and sampling Draino or bleach. They are also attracted to the sweetened insect poisons such as ant paste which often contains arsenic. They can electrocute themselves by poking things into electrical outlets or by chewing through light cords. They can pull irons over on themselves or, while sitting in grandmother's lap, will grab her cup of hot coffee and get burned. In the case of crawling babies and toddlers the house *must* be baby proofed.

Grandparents who remember what little ones are like at that stage of life will put up their prize possessions. The beautiful table lamp has a cord just made to pull on. The table cloth hanging down within reach looks like a great hand-hold to use to pull one's self up into a standing position.

Jeremy

Jeremy was two-years-old and a precocious talker. But Grandmother and her daughter were rather good talkers too. They were busy bringing each other up to date on events in their lives and didn't pay much attention to Jeremy. The table was set for dinner, although luckily the hot food had not been put on yet. Jeremy toddled over to the table, grabbed the table cloth to try to pull himself up higher so he could see what was on the table. The table cloth, and all that was on it, slid off onto Jeremy who fell down along with a clatter of breaking dishes. Mother and grandmother both gasped, then ran into the dining room. Jeremy was setting wide eyed but fortunately uninjured among a mess of dishes, some intact and some broken. He looked up at mother and grandmother and excitedly announced, "I boke a dish! I see 'em coming!"

When they get older, incidents like Jeremy's become less amusing. Grandparents have the right to declare some rooms and many things off limits to grandchildren. The limits should be discussed with the parents first, and then clearly explained to the grandchildren. The explanation should be followed with action, the neutral discipline discussed earlier in this book.

Tom and Jerry

Tom and Jerry weren't the comic book characters so often pictured in the cartoon movies tearing up the house. They were Grandmother's three- and five-year-old grandsons. But when they first visited Grandma felt that they must have taken lessons from the cartoon Tom and Jerry. The family had just driven across the country for this special visit to Grandma's. While she and her daughter and son-in-law greeted each other the boys each unloaded a bag of toys they had brought and then proceeded to leave a trail of disorder through the house. Grandmother winced, and said to their parents, "The boys have to run off some of their pent-up energy after that car ride. But I had better lay down some ground rules about where they can play in the house, don't you think? I'll take them into the back yard now and after they run around some and have played a bit, I'll tell them which rooms they can play in and about keeping things picked up. Their grandpa bought an outdoor game for them to play on the lawn. I think that they will enjoy it."

Naturally the boy's parents agreed. After Tom and Jerry had run off some of their frustrations and stored-up energy from the long auto trip, Grandmother took them on a tour of the house. She told them which rooms were off limits to them and advised them that she did not stand for toys left around on the floor because people might trip on them. Grandfather brought a box into the family room and told the boys to put their toys in the box each time they finished playing with them. He said, "If you are too tired to put the toys away after you finish playing with them, and that means before you go outside each time, then I'll figure that you are too tired to use the toys for a few days and I will put them away where you can't get them until you learn to put them where they belong yourself. Now, what do you say? Would your Mother and Father let me take you down town to the ice cream store?"

Naturally the boys soon forgot. Grandfather said nothing but picked up the toys and put them in a closet where they couldn't get them. When the boys asked where their toys were, Gramps said, "Well, you are too tired to play with them so I put them away. Remember the rules? Meanwhile why don't we go out on the lawn and I'll show you how to play croquet." The lesson was learned and the boys soon figured out that Grandma and Grandpa meant what they said. They soon began picking up their toys.

Children's visits are more welcome when they learn to follow Grandma's rules at Grandma's house. Going to Grandma's is a good way for children to learn about being a welcome visitor in someone else's home. For example, Bella, age three comes to call on Grandma frequently because she lives close by. Bella heads straight for her toy box under the piano in the living room and pulls out the picture books and toy farm animals. She has learned where her toys are and that the place to play is in the living room, not all over the house. She entertains herself well for one her age and is careful before leaving to pick up everything and put it away for the next time.

Bella's six-year-old sister, Beth, likes to use Grandpa's computer. She has learned to use programs to compose music, write, play games, draw and paint. She also enjoys practicing on the piano. She too is a welcome visitor because she has learned to ask permission and be careful how she uses Grandpa's things. In this way, grandparent's homes can be another kind and friendly place where children can both explore and learn how to be good visitors. No wonder Grandma and Grandpa have a warm and loving relationship with Bella, Beth and their Mother and Father.

The Neighborhood

Neighborhoods are an extension of the home environment. Some are really clusters of apartments and others are groups of houses. In either case children need a friendly caring neighborhood with good personal and community values and neighbors who are not afraid to protect, to stimulate, to praise — and to say no. The neighborhood should offer a structure — a sense of permanence, of acceptance, of community agreed-upon standards for children to obey. The neighborhood needs adults, including grandparents, to observe, to protect, to insist on adherence to common community standards. It should have adults, including grandparents, who lead, play, stimulate, educate, and teach good values by example and by demand. In a good neighborhood people have a mutual sense of obligation. This starts with neighbors becoming acquainted with each other and becoming aware of each others' strengths and needs. Many grandparents have the time and the talent to be the social catalysts required to change a block of apartments or houses into a neighborhood.

Communities

Beyond neighborhoods, communities have their own effects and represent another step in the process of teaching children about the world they live in. The first step is family, including grandparents, giving a sense of belonging and a feeling of security. The next step is the neighborhood, offering structure and caring with opportunity and limits, expanding the sense of belonging and reinforcing the sense of security. Communities, large or small clusters of neighborhoods, places for people to live and work, offer the next step.

The small community, a town or village of less than 50,000 people offers a microcosm of human function, an advanced lesson in what society is all about. Relationships start in the small town family by including the children as helpers at home or in the store after school. The children know the judge, were kissed by the mayor during the election campaign, and become acquainted with the plumber and fireman, the doctor and the mailman. They know where Dad works and what he does. They learn who and what it takes to keep a community functioning.

People in small towns are mutually dependent on each other and their customs reflect the needs of its people. Children who grow up in these little communities have a marvelous opportunity to see how people live together on a community basis. They observe each adult at work, learn how men and women treat each other in differing situations and learn the rules children are expected to live by. By the age of ten, most children in a small community have a clear picture of life in their community, the roles people play and the values and rules that induce success or failure. The basic stuff of life exists in such communities — and children absorb it.

By contrast, a child living in a twenty-fourth floor condominium in Manhattan finds it a challenge to reach school and return from it each day. Traveling to a friend's house can be complicated enough or unsafe enough that parents often have to take them. They can only travel at certain times because of the public transportation schedules. This child rarely knows any of the men and women in his own building, let alone dignitaries or workers whose functions enable a large city like New York to operate.

Is it possible for such a city boy or girl to understand how a community really works? Their image of life and the operation of society is fragmented and incomplete. This lack of a full understanding of the operation of society may have important implications for the future. Young men and women raised in a small town, where they could experience the whole picture, sometimes seem better able to rise to high positions in industry or politics, probably because they have experienced and understand the overall scope of community operations. The relationships, values and principles they learned while young enable them to handle a much larger scale of community or industrial operations. The child in the condominium is stuck with a distorted model of community and may not be able to adapt this image to the demands of high office or broad responsibilities. In tomorrow's world an even greater understanding of how people can work together toward a common goal will be needed.

Many grandparents today were reared in small towns or villages. They are able to help city-reared children understand many of the functions of society hidden from them by the complexity of city life. Trips to the dump, to the City Hall, to the printers and the newspaper offices, to the police station and the garage all help broaden a child's perspectives. Taking them to the small town where grandfather was raised may make an indelible impression on young minds. Talking about these and many other natural life experiences helps children understand their world. Memories are precious, and sharing them is teaching. A child's understanding about the world, its values, and its ways can be broadened by tales of everyday life in the past. Personal history is always more engaging than the generalities presented in history books. Help your grandchildren feel connected to the past, to feel their roots by sharing family stories that have been handed down. It is important for your grandchildren to hear these stories and only you can provide that sense of actually having been there. Here are a few examples:

Butch

Great-grandfather's nickname was Butch because when he was a young man he delivered meat from the market to Mrs. Winchester. This confused old lady, the widow of the owner of the Winchester rifle factory, thought that the spirits of all those killed by Winchester guns were haunting her. As a result she kept a crew of carpenters working twenty-four hours a day making spirit traps so her San Jose mansion would be safe. Butch drove the butcher wagon, pulled by a team of horses, to the mansion every day — it took a lot of food to keep all those carpenters full!

Frank

Grandfather Frank LaKamp came across the plains in a covered wagon when he was eight-years-old. Glenn remembered the stories of that great adventure, told by the open fireplace on winter nights before televisions was ever dreamed of. Except for the driver, the entire family walked most of the way to spare the oxen. One of Frank's jobs was to gather wood on the way so they would have enough for a fire when they stopped that night. The wagon broke down while they were lowering it over a cliff on the western slope of the Rocky Mountains in Colorado in the Ute Indian Territory. They made one of the first dwellings in what was to become the town of Meeker. Frank's father was a tailor, a neighbor who came in the wagon train with them was a blacksmith and another was a carpenter. Together, sharing and exchanging work, they started a town. During that time Frank remembered that the Utes were helpful to the settlers.

Ralph

Grandfather Ralph walked with a limp. When he was a young man in Placerville, a small town in California, he took a job as a deputy sheriff. The town bully was especially mean when he was drunk and he would occasionally shoot up his house and beat his wife. Ralph was called to go arrest him one evening when his shots were endangering his neighbors. In the process the bully shot Ralph in the leg, but Ralph grabbed his gun and forced him to drop it, arrested him and took him to jail. Then he went to the town doctor. He had to pay for his own care because no medical insurance existed in those times. And because of his wound he couldn't do his job as a deputy so the Town Council fired him. His family cared for him and he eventually recovered.

Lilly

Grandmother Lilly never lost her Kentucky hillbilly twang. Even though she lived in a suburb of Dayton, Ohio, with her daughter's family, she always insisted each spring on going to the country and buying crates full of fruit. Then the house would be full of steam and sweet smells while she canned the fruit in Mason jars. Her grandchildren would bring their friends over to sample her home canned fruit. They would look, wide eyed, at the shelves full of peaches, cherries, jellies and jams. It was sort of a home supermarket. As Lilly dished out jam for their sandwiches she would recollect about stringing shuck beans on the front porch of their cabin in Appalachia, and about how her husband Kermit used to leave at five in the morning for the coal mine where he worked and would get back, coughing up black coal dust tinged sputum, around six in the evening because it took so long to get down into the mine where he could start his eight hour shift.

Is Your Grandchild Growing Up In The City?

The rapid growth of modern cities, especially following World War II, ignored some primary needs of children and youth in spite of the widespread belief that they need a good environment. City growth in industrialized nations was generally unplanned and haphazard. No philosophy or political ideology guided growth except how each individual could benefit himself under the circumstances. Developers and land owners could make more money by building shopping malls than apartments and more for homes than parks. City planners were hard pressed just to build streets and sewers fast enough. Prime flat farm land was gobbled up because it was easier to build on. As suburbia engulfed the countryside the traffic problems became worse and worse. Families moved to the new suburbs in the periphery of the city to be able to afford a house, only to be faced with hour-long commutes each way to work. These commutes will get longer if current estimates are right that the amount of traffic will double in the next three decades!

Cities seem to be built for the dollar rather than for people. Certainly a relationship exists between people's needs and the dollars they spend. But either the dreams are too big or the numbers of dollars many young families earn are too little for them to afford to buy a house, or even rent one near their work. The question seems to come down to choices between houses, commuting and children. The urban/suburban sprawl doesn't seem to do a very good job of meeting the needs of the people who live and work there.

Constantinos A. Doxiadis, a far-seeing modern Greek city planner, proposed that cities should be supportive to all the human beings living there. He felt that cities should be built to meet the needs of people rather than forcing people into the straight jacket of the city. It is doubtful that he considered two hour commutes, uninspired apartment box dwellings and no playgrounds for children as meeting the needs of the inhabitants. Ecologists are well advised to give some attention to the ecology of urban and suburban dwellers, especially their children. Doxiadis did. He established the field of ekistics, the science of human settlements, with the concept that properly built cities can play a positive role in the development of the inhabitants.

We, as grandparents, need to examine our values and priorities. The human life span includes an "ekistic" line. Winston Churchill said, "First we shape our cities, and then our cities shape us." Mankind must live with the environment and when it is a man made environment, a town or city, it should be designed or remodeled to favor its residents. Particularly important, in our opinion, is a design that supports children, youth and their families. This requires major grass roots political action. Many grandparents have been turned off by the mechanics of politics and a good number don't even bother to vote. But the attention of the elders to the development of their city or town may be a crucial and invaluable legacy for the future. Our grandchildren should be able to roam open fields like many of us did as children. They should be raised in communities that value children, stimulate them and help, rather than hinder, their development. We grandparents have a lot to do.

COMMUNITY GRANDPARENTS

Where you live obviously has a lot to do with whether or not you can have the amount of contact with your grandchildren that they need. However, where you live needn't interfere with their peers. You can have a significant impact on the generation that will take over the reins of society early in the next century. The importance of this input to both the young and the old cannot be overemphasized. Children growing up without exposure to the elderly may be less secure than they might have been. They will lack that extra self-esteem that comes from the attention and approval of one's elders. Grandparents can, as we saw in earlier chapters, help this upcoming generation become more competent and socially responsible.

For the old, aside from the innate rewards that come from close association with the young, there are other practical aspects to be considered. Children growing up away from their elders have less empathy for the old than those in families who include the elders in daily life. Empathy may be especially needed early in the next century when there will be only two wage earners supporting each Social Security recipient. The stress of supporting the upcoming huge population of the elderly may overwhelm and threaten the system.

Paul R. Ehrlich and Anna H. Ehrlich, authors of, *The Population Explosion,* 1990, feel that some in the United States ignore environmental protection with the philosophy "get ours now and the hell with posterity." This lack of respect for future generations helps explain why an affluent twenty-one-year-old surfer in Southern California was quoted by the New York Times as saying, "This is the '90s man. We're the type of people who don't take no for an answer. If your mom says no to a kid in the '90s, the kid's just going to laugh." Such mutual lack of respect between the generations bodes ill for the future. Fortunately both attitudes represent extremes. Still, the withering of values represented by such attitudes reflects some reality.

It becomes increasingly critical for the senior generation, whether grandparents or not, to take positive action and bridge the gap between the generations; teach youth to respect their elders by showing them that elders respect youth. One very positive way is to join the trend of communities to become a Kid's Place. This concept of cities designed for people, including the kids, grew out of a visit by Dr. Aldrich to the famous Greek architect and city planner Constantinos A. Doxiadis on an island in the Greek Peloponese.

Kid'sPlace: An Idea Hatched

Dr. Aldrich, a professor of pediatrics with a deep interest in anthropology, visited Doxiadis who was at the time completing his classic book, *EKISTICS*. Dr. Aldrich asked what the book was about and Doxiadis replied, "It is about cities for people." One of the world's leading city planners, Doxiadis knew that cities can shape the development of human beings — they are more than simply clusters of buildings and services. Dr. Aldrich, whose focus was on human growth and development and on children, suggested that such a city could be developed into a very good place to raise children, and that it was time to put this concept into action.

Doxiadis was invited by civic leaders looking for guidance for the future development of Seattle to lecture about public planning. Dr. Aldrich asked him how to design a city that also fostered the growth and development of children and youth. Doxiadis did not respond at the time but later invited Aldrich to participate with others, some of whom were grandparents, in the Delos Symposion aboard a ship in the Mediterranean. The others included famous intellectuals such as Buckminster Fuller, Arnold Toynbee and Margaret Mead. With this wise and intelligent group of men and women, Aldrich was able to develop the concept of Kid'sPlace. Utilizing experience and knowledge from such diverse disciplines as architecture, sociology and psychology and travelling to other cultures to see how they provided for their children, the concept took shape.

Seattle's Kid'sPlace Project planning started in 1983 when civic leaders noted a sharp decline in the number of children living in Seattle. A group of citizens discussed the powerful implication of this drop in the number of Seattle's children. They decided that the time was right to make Seattle "a great place for kids." This private sector initiative was joined by Mayor Charles Royer who brought many volunteer organizations together with the city government to form an organization called "Kid'sPlace."

Within a year an effective lobby of volunteers from youth agencies, community organizations, city schools, government departments, businesses, industries, colleges and universities had created a kid's lobby for Seattle. Many of the volunteers were grandparents.

Kid'sPlace Programs

Undoubtedly, the most far reaching early step taken by Kid's Place was *The Mayor's Survey of 1984.* The opinions of school children in private and public schools were solicited using questionnaires filled out by the children. Their views, taken from over 6,000 responses, clearly showed that what parents thought their children were thinking was not always the case. The survey brought to light some major children and youth issues that needed to be addressed. The children took the study seriously. They wanted a safe, clean, beautiful city with more things for children to do and places to go.

The children zeroed in on a limited number of items, the most significant being schools (helpful but boring), environment (needed to be cleaned up), safety in downtown areas (they felt it was dangerous), and Seattle Center (best place in town for children to go with or without parents). Their high rating for parks and the Seattle Center (former site of the 1964 World's Fair) made such an impact on the adult community that it resulted in major improvements that are continuing today. One part of the survey invited children to apply to be Mayor for a day. Selection of a winner was made on the basis of the originality of the child's response to the question: "If I were Mayor, the first thing I would do for children is ?"

The 12 year old girl, winner of the competition, made a lasting impression on the media when she appeared at a press conference starting her day as the Mayor. Her poise and sophistication before reporters from the press, radio and TV was mentioned in their cordial editorials and reports. It reminded the public of how aware, intelligent and capable children of this age group can be. It raised public awareness of the needs of children.

Coincident with the Mayor's Survey, four more initiatives were undertaken:

- To create an action plan for the city.
- To hold a national conference on children in cities.
- To establish a Youth Board.
- To have an annual celebration, "Kid's Day," in recognition of Seattle children and youth.

Implementing the Kid'sPlace Program

A *Kid's Board* was established. Thirty teenagers drawn from the pool of applicants to be Mayor for a day formed the Board taking staggered terms of 1, 2, and 3 year appointments. The Kid's Board is a youth leadership program to allow middle school and high school students the opportunity to exert leadership in the community. As terms end, the Board members select new members. City policy proposals are brought to the Kid's Board by the Mayor and these are not limited to issues about children and youth. Many actions resulted including a national conference on Looking at Cities With Children In Mind, an annual Kid's Day in Seattle, and a bevy of research projects on families and children.

A *Kid'sPlace Action Agenda* was developed by six citizen task forces composed of volunteers carefully chosen to be representative for age, sex, race, and neighborhood. The 250 men and women prepared an agenda of 30 action items ranging from the arts, recreation, housing, child care, schools, information availability, health, to government. The agenda has been implemented in most areas. We recommend it to other cities primarily because it brings citizens of all ages together around a central value, their children and youth. It is a non-partisan political process of sharing ideas and stimulating actions. We believe that metropolitan communities will find the Kid'sPlace approach to be effective and that people involved will enjoy the experience and satisfactions. It is also fun.

THE NEED FOR GRANDPARENTS

Children need friendly cities. More than that, they need involved grandparents who offer love, security, continuity and meaning. In a world of change and challenge on a planet where our life-friendly environment is threatened, children especially need the security of continuity to help them face the future with confidence. They also need the knowledge and wisdom which grandparents can impart, the history of both personal and community achievements and errors. Grandparents offer a model of maturity, compassion and experience; they can be imitated and they challenge the child to live up to his or her potential. Children absorb the lessons of the past through the ancestral roots which their grandparents represent. This gives an up close and personal look at some of the values of the past which can help them successfully meet the future.

Grandparents tend to underestimate their importance to their grandchildren. Simply knowing that they have or had grandparents means more to children than most think. Adopted children, for example, often fantasize about who their "real" parents and grandparents are — an example of the need of humans for continuity to give their life more meaning and importance.

However basic the need for continuity, today's children need much more. To become confident, competent and socially responsible citizens they need good parenting and sensible grandparenting. As we have seen, experience tends to make grandparents more rational and authoritative; it makes them better parents than they probably were when they were younger. This allows them to back up and occasionally supplement their adult-child's and spouse's parenting efforts. They do this wisely by modeling diplomatic action. The action usually takes the form of neutral rewards and discipline using the values of cooperation and consensus. The rewards given to adult-children and grandchildren are powerful. They include the attention, respect and concern which validate the importance of the child and his parents. The relationship offers the security of being around surviving ancestors, the practical support grandparents offer and the fun and satisfaction inherent in such association. Such rewards make grandparents quite effective in their efforts to improve the lives of their grandchildren. The rewards also work well for elders relating to neighborhood and community youth. Rarely does the need exist for any negative disciplinary action except for the withdrawal of the rewards.

The Need For Happy Grandparents

Another need of children deserves emphasis. They need content and happy grandparents who hopefully have retained a sense of humor. This contentment can come from the rewards innate in grandparenting. Enjoying grandparenting represents part of the reward. Most grandparents snort with derision if someone offers to tell them how to enjoy their grandchildren. We all recognize that the rewards of being around grandchildren and our adult-children come in many different colors. A look at various rewards bestowed on grandparents by their grandchildren, aside from candy smeared kisses, offers interesting perspectives. We react from the heart with love, that's a given reward. Other rewards include three broad categories: pride, fun and security.

It's the rare and unfortunate grandparent who doesn't feel the swell of joy in the chest when viewing the spanking-new baby grandchild or when attending the graduation of that grandchild from college. Those biological ties that bind cannot be denied. Whether its the eyes of the newborn or the smarts of an up and coming young engineer or police officer, grandparents generally take some of the credit. Rightly so, some of those genes came from us! In a way grandchildren represent immortality. That's comforting to grandparents. Almost all grandparents approached during the writing of this book were eager to tell the world about just how enjoyable it is to be a grandparent.

Grandchildren also reward their grandparents with respect. They instinctively know that growing old takes more than luck. Survivors have courage, strength, determination and wisdom. We made our mistakes and usually learned from them. Time has worn off our rough edges leaving most of us with an admirable patina which enhances, if not exaggerates, our achievements and strengths. Grandparents offer a model of continuity and roots, an elder that the young can look up to and admire.

As survivors we can distill and pass on some of those lessons we learned to help our grandchildren avoid some of the errors we made in the past. More importantly, we can offer a positive outlook on life and build our grandchildren's hopes and self esteem. In the process we develop personally. We learn to recognize (if we didn't before) that we are worthy of self-respect. By contributing to our grandchildren's confidence and competency we improve their lives. This effect ripples throughout the world. The results establish and confirm our own importance.

By planting good values that will serve mankind well in this upcoming 21st Century, including the seeds of logic and compassion, of willpower and love, we help our grandchildren become responsible citizens. In doing so, no grandparent is insignificant. All of us have a role with our grandchildren. We made their lives possible; if we didn't exist neither would they. We enhance the meaning of the family and we will each live a little bit in our grandchildren.

Grandchildren want us. Oh sure, there are times when they may selfishly ignore us. Some, from temperament or from environment, may not be the loving, accepting and obedient type of grandchildren we want. But grandparents have been around long enough to recognize that this too shall change. As people grow they evolve. Stages of negativism and selfishness often pass — are outgrown with experience. Lack of appreciation today does not mean we won't be appreciated in the future. Just as we become wiser with age, so will they. Just as we learn that selfishness doesn't lead to happiness, so will they.

GRANDCHILDREN ARE GOD'S WAY OF COMPENSATING FOR GROWING OLD!

Most of us became grandparents without much thought. We react from the heart. Few lessons existed except for our personal experiences with our own grandparents or with other grandparents we manage to run across. The many aspects of grandparenting covered in this book offer some concepts which we hope will increase your enjoyment of this entrancing occupation. We freely acknowledge that we have drawn on the wisdom and experience of hundreds of grandparents like you to bring this book together.

One basic lesson these hundreds of grandparents taught stands out — grandparenting rewards the most to those who invest in it the most.

REFERENCES/READINGS

CHAPTER 1

A New Agenda for a Weary Empire, George F. Kennan, Stanford Magazine, Dec. 1989. (Excert reprinted with permission.)

Grandparenting, Understanding Today's Children, David Elkind, Scott, Foresman and Company, Glenview, Illinois, 1990. (Excerpts reprinted with permission.)

Grandparents/Grandchildren—The Vital Connection, Arthur Kornhaber, M.D. and Kenneth L. Woodward, Anchor Press/Doubleday, Garden City, NY 1981.

Vital Connections—The Grandparenting Newsletter, Dr. Arthur Kornhaber, Editor, Foundation For Grandparenting, P.O. Box 31 Lake Placid, NY 12946 ($20.00/year tax deductible). (Exerpt reprinted with permission.)

The Path to Power—The Years of Lyndon Johnson, Robert A. Caro, Vintage, Random House of Canada, Toronto, 1983.

The Common Sense Book of Baby and Child Care, Benjamin Spock, M.D., Duell, Sloan and Pearce, NY, 1946.

Hold Them Very Close, Then Let Them Go, Richard Robertiello, M.D., Dial Press, NY, 1975.

Families In Peril, Marian Wright Edelman, Harvard University Press, Cambridge, 1987.

Kids First Newsletter—Parents Lobbying for Children, Lakeview Postal Outlet, P.O. Box 36032, 6449 Crowchild Trail, S.W. Calgary, Alberta, Canada T3E7C6 — Membership Fee $10.00/year. (Excerpt reprinted with permission.)

The Search For Structure. A Report on American Youth Today. Francis A.J. Ianni, The Free Press, A Division of MacMillan, Inc., New York, 1989.

The Survival Of The Wisest, Jonas Salk, Harer & Row, New York, 1973.

Environment and Population: Problems of Adaptation, An Experimental Book Integrating Statements by 162 Contributors, Edited and Integrated by John B. Calhoun, Praeger Publishers, NY 1983.

Lifeboat Ethics, A Radical Approach, Garrett Hardin, in Global Hinder: *A Look at the Problem and Potential Solutions,* Fobers and Merrill editors, University of Evansville Press, Evansville, IN 1986.

Plight of the Ik and Karadilt is Seen As A Chilling Possible End For Man, John B. Calhoun, Smithsonian Magazine, Nov. 1972.

The Biocultural Basis Of Health, Lorna G. Moore, Peter W. Van Arsdale, JoAnn E. Glittenberg, Robert A. Aldrich, The Waveland Press, Inc., Prospect Heights, Illinois, 1987.

The Social Context of Change, Robert A. Aldrich, Psychiatric Annals, 16(10), October, 1986, pp. 613–618.

The Nature Of A Humane Society, Editor H. Ober Hess, Fortress Press, Philadelphia, 1977, pages 171–185.

Within Our Reach, Lisbeth B. Schorr with Daniel Schorr, Anchor Press, New York, 1988.

CHAPTER 2

The Parents' Guide to Child Raising, Glenn Austin, M.D., Prentice Hall, Inc., Englewood Cliffs, NJ, 07632, 1978. (Excerpts reprinted with permission.)

Birthrights, Richard Farson, Macmillan Publishing Co, Inc., NY, 1974.

The Strong Willed Child, Dr. James Dobson, Tyndale House Publishers, Inc., Wheaton, IL 60187.

Parent Effectiveness Training, Thomas Gordon, Peter H. Wyden, Inc., NY, 1970.

Love and Power—Parent and Child: How To Raise Competent, Confident Children, Glenn Austin, M.D., Robert Erdmann Publishing, Incline Village, NV, 1988. (Excerpts reprinted with permission.)

Antecedents of Self-Esteem, Stanley Coopersmith, W.H. Freeman and Co., NY, 1967.

Educating the Infant and Toddler, Burton White, Ph.D., Lexington Books, D.C. Heath and Co., Lexington, MA, 1988. (Excerpts reprinted with permission.)

The First Three Years of Life, Burton L. White, Prentice Hall, Englewood Cliffs, NJ, 1975.

Evaluation of an Early Parent Education Program, Early Childhood Research Quarterly, 1989.

New Parents as Teachers Project, Evaluation Report Summary, Arthur L. Mallory, Commissioner of Education, Missouri State Board of Education, Jefferson City, Missouri 65102, 1985.

How to Avoid Your Parent's Mistakes When You Raise Your Childen, Claudette Wassil-Grimm, Pocket Books, NY, NY, 1990. *(Excerpts reprinted with permission.)*

CHAPTER 3

The Psychological Theory of Neurosis, Otto Fenichel, M.D., W.W. Norton and Company, NY, 1985 (1945?)

Your Inner Child of the Past, W. Hugh Missildine, Simon and Schuster, NY, 1963.

Love and Power—Parent and Child, ibid Chapter 2.

CHAPTER 4

Babies Are Human Beings, C.A. Aldrich and Mary M. Aldrich, The Macmillan Co., NY, 1938.

The Importance Of Infancy, Lawrence K. Frank, Random House, NY, 1966.

What Every Baby Knows, T. Berry Brazelton, M.D., Addison-Wesley Publishing Company, Reading, MA, 1987.

Research on Support for Parents and Infants in the Postnatal Period, Cowan, Philip A. and Cowan, Carolyn P., Ablex Publishing, NJ, 1989.

Couple Relationships, Parenting Styles and the Child's Development at Three, Cowan, P.A. and Cowan, C.P., Paper presented to the Society for Research in Child Development, April, 1967 (The Cowans are in the Department of Psychology, University of California, Berkeley).

The Nature of The Child, Jerome Kagan, Basic Books, NY, 1984.

Punishment, Gary C. Walters and Joan E. Grusec, W.H. Freeman and Company, San Francisco, 1977.

Love and Power, Ibid, Chapter 2.

The First Three Years of Life, Ibid, Chapter 2.

CHAPTER 5

The Long Distance Grandmother, Selma Wasserman, Hartley & Marks, Inc., Point Roberts, WA, 1988.

Love and Power, Ibid, Chapter 2.

The Search for Structure, Ibid, Chapter 1.

The Biocultural Basis Of Health, Ibid, Chapter 1.

CHAPTER 6

Building the House of Marriage, William Summers, M.D., Robert Erdmann Publishing, Incline Villae, NV, 1990. (Excerpts reprinted with permission.)

How to Avoid Your Parents' Mistakes When You Raise Your Children, Ibid, Chapter 2.

Love and Power, Ibid, Chapter 2.

CHAPTER 7

Ex Familia, Colleen Leahy Johnson, Ph.D., Rutgers University Press, New Brunswick, NJ, 1988.

Active and Latent Functions of Grandparenting During the Divorce Process, Colleen Leahy Johnson, Ph.D., The Gerontologist, Vol 28 No 2, 1988.

The Motherhood Report, Louis Genevie and Eve Margoliez, Macmillan Publishing Co, New York, 1987. (Excerpts reprinted with permission.)

Second Chances, Judith Wallerstein, Ph.D., and Sandra Blakeslee, Ticknor and Fields, 1989. (Excerpts reprinted with permission.)

CHAPTER 8

How to Avoid Your Parents' Mistakes When You Raise Your Children, Ibid, Chapter 2.

The New Realities, Peter F. Drucker, Harper & Row, NY, 1989.

Plagues and Peoples, William H. NcNeill, Anchor Press, Garden City, NY, 1976.

Women Who Love Too Much, Robin Norwood, Jeremy P. Tarcher, Inc., NY, 1985.

Anger, The Misunderstood Emotion, Carol Tavris, Simon and Schuster, 1982.

Your Inner Child of the Past, Hugh Missildine, M.D., Simon and Schuster, NY, 1963.

Love and Power, Ibid, Chapter 2.

Variations on a Theme, Jo Seligmann, Newsweek Winter/Spring, 1990, Special Issue. (Excerpts reprinted with permission.)

Grandparents Raising Grandchildren, P.O. Box 104, Colleyville, Texas, 76034, phone (817) 577-0435.

House of Marriage, Ibid, Chapter 6.

CHAPTER 9

Family Affairs Newsletter, **Institute for American Values, 250 West 57th Street, Suite 2415, New York City, 10107, (212) 246-3942.**

The Family in America Newsletter, **Rockford, Institute Center on the Family in America, Subscription Department, P.O. Box 416, Mt. Morris, IL, 61054.**

"Welcome Home", **Publication of Mothers at Home, P.O. Box 2208, Merrifield, VA 22116 ($15.00/year U.S., $18.00/year Canada and Mexico, $25.00/year overseas).**

Toward a National Policy for Children and Families, the National Research Council, National Academy of Sciences, Washington, D.C., 1976.

"Becoming Attached," Robert Karen, The Atlantic Monthly, Feb. 1990.

When School is Out and Nobody's Home, Coolsen, Seligson and Gabardino, National Committee for Prevention of Child Abuse, 332 South Michigan Avenue Suite 950, Chicago, IL 60604. Excerpts reprinted with permission. (Available by mail for $4.50 from NCPCA).

Meanwhile. . . Back To The Child, Elizabeth Kjorlaug Wolfe, Car-Mel Publishers, San Diego, CA, 1987. (Excerpts reprinted with permission.)

Variations On A Theme: The 21st Century Family, Newsweek, Winter/Spring issue, 1990. (Exerts reprinted with permission.)

Johnny Still Can't Read—But You Can Teach Him at Home, Kaathryn Diehl and G.K. Hodenfield, Reading Reform Foundation, 1517 South Clifton, Bloomington, IN, 47401, 1977.

Grandparenting, Ibid, Chapter 1.

Understanding Mental Retardation, James F. Kavanagh, Paul H. Brookes, Publisher, Baltimore, 1988.

Developmental Variations and Learning Disorders, Melvin D. Levine, M.D., Educators Publishing Service, Cambridge, 1987.

CHAPTER 10

Kid'sPlace address: Executive Director, Seattle's Kid'sPlace, 158 Thomas Street—Suite 14, Seattle, WA 98109.

Kid'sPlace — Seattle, USA, Robert A. Aldrich, Ekistics, July-August, 1987.

Ekistics, Constantinos A. Doxiadis, Hutchinson of London, Publisher, 1968.

Anthropopolis, City for Human Development, C.A. Doxiadis et al, a symposion. Athens Publishing Center (Greece), 24 Stratiotikou Syndesmou, Athens 136, Greece. A great classic available in many libraries, published in English, 1974.

Home, Ibid, Chapter 6.

The Child In The World Of Tomorrow, Spyros Doxiadis, Editor Jaqueline Tyrwhitt, Executive Editor, Pergamon Press, NY, 1979.

The Economy of Cities, Jane Jacobs, Random House, NY, 1969.

INDEX